Learning by Voting

Learning by Voting

Sequential Choices in Presidential Primaries and Other Elections

Rebecca B. Morton
and
Kenneth C. Williams

Ann Arbor
THE UNIVERSITY OF MICHIGAN PRESS

Copyright © by the University of Michigan 2001
All rights reserved
Published in the United States of America by
The University of Michigan Press
Manufactured in the United States of America
♾ Printed on acid-free paper

2004   2003   2002   2001   4   3   2   1

A CIP catalog record for this book is available from the British Library.

Library of Congress Cataloging-in-Publication Data

Morton, Rebecca B., 1954–
      Learning by voting : sequential choices in presidential primaries and other
   elections / Rebecca B. Morton and Kenneth C. Williams.
            p.   cm.
      Includes bibliographical references and index.
      ISBN 0-472-11129-9 (cloth : alk. paper)
      1. Primaries—United States.   2. Presidents—United States—Nomination.
   3. Voting—United States.   I. Williams, Kenneth C.   II. Title.

   JK522 .M67   2001
   324.5'4'0973—dc21   2001027071

Contents

Figures and Tables

Acknowledgments

Experimental research like ours is not possible without support—financial, institutional, and personal. We are exceedingly grateful for the funding that we have received from Michigan State University and the National Science Foundation to conduct our experiments. We appreciate the use of the computer laboratories at Michigan State University. On a personal level, we thank Terry Conklin, who supplied the computer software for our experiments, Reneé Agress and Sara McLaughlin for their invaluable assistance in recruiting subjects and running the experiments, and Kristin Kanthak for her research assistance. We have presented this research at a number of locations in the last few years—Arizona State University, the Hoover Institution at Stanford University, University of Michigan, University of California, Santa Barbara, Ohio State University, Princeton University, University of California, Los Angeles, the 1998 Public Choice Meetings, and the 1996 Midwest Political Science Associate Meetings in Chicago, and we value highly the comments from participants at these presentations. We have also benefited from the helpful observations and aid of the anonymous reviewers of our work as well as those from Paul Abramson, James Adams, Janet Box-Steffensmeier, Nancy Burns, Charles Cameron, Marcie Cowley, Cary Covington, Mark Fey, Ada Finifter, Elisabeth Gerber, Tobin Grant, Charles Myers, Jonathan Nagler, Marta Nelson, Emerson Niou, Philip Paolino, Charles Shipan, Peverill Squire, Robert Stein, Michael Traugott, and Rick Wilson. Finally, we thank our families for their support and especially their patience as we completed this project.

CHAPTER 1

Sequence and Making Votes Count

The Perils of Dates

The 2000 presidential primary season was one of the fastest seasons to date. The major party nominees had virtually secured the nomination approximately five weeks after the primaries began. The short time frame of the primary season was not a coincidence; rather, it was a result of concerted efforts by some states to exert influence over the outcome by moving their primary or caucus to an earlier calendar date. The desire for states to "front-load" the primary season to increase their influence has evolved over a period of time and caught momentum after the 1996 election. Consider the following that occurred in Missouri—similar situations likely occurred in each of the other states that moved their primaries to an earlier date.

In early May 1998, Missouri state senator Ronnie DePasco realized that he had made a miscalculation. He had put forward a bill to change Missouri from a state that chooses delegates for presidential nominating conventions via caucuses to one with presidential primaries. The bill seemed to have promise at first; the current system had been criticized for low voter participation. And DePasco proposed that the new primary election be held the same day as municipal elections in April, which would decrease costs. The bill passed the state senate and the House Committee on Elections. However, it faced trouble once it reached the floor of the Missouri house. Critics argued that April would be too late for a presidential primary to be worthwhile. After all, in 1996 California's primary was held on March 26. If the presidential nominations "were still up for grabs in late March, delegate-rich California would essentially end the contest and render any state with a later primary date politically moot as a presidential player," political analysts pointed out.[1] DePasco's bill faltered for scheduling Missouri's primary after California.

Ironically, just two weeks after DePasco's bill toppled in the Missouri house, California state senator Jim Costa's bill moving California's presidential primary for 2000 to the first Tuesday in March (two weeks earlier than in 1996, and the earliest allowable date under Democratic rules), was approved by the California state senate (scheduling the primary earlier than even Missouri legislators believed it would be). State senators in California contended that their primary in 1996 had been too late to influence the nomination process. The Associated Press reported:

> Sen. Bill Lockyer, D-Hayward, said the earlier primary was appealing because "I don't like the fact that New Hampshire and Iowa don't represent the depth and breadth of this country and they have a disproportionate influence." . . . Lockyer said presidential candidates come to California to use it like a political ATM machine to finance their campaigns in states with earlier primaries. They may pay more attention to California voters if the primary is earlier, Lockyer said. But, he added, there is a down side to moving up the primary. An early California primary helps incumbents and the wealthy, he said. "You'll renominate the retreads and the rich—they'll run in the largest state."[2] (May 15, 1998)

Eventually Missouri and several other states moved their primaries to match the delegate heavyweights, California and New York, creating "Super Tuesday" on March 7. On that date alone, 26.8 percent of Republican delegates and 37.2 percent of Democratic delegates were at stake. The influence that this attracts may continue to prompt more and more states to move their primaries closer to the beginning of the primary season, resulting in front-loading the presidential primary season into a "virtual" national primary (Balz 1993). Numerous state leaders advocate moving their primaries because they believe the current system gives undue influence to nonrepresentative early voters.

But some policymakers, like California state senator Lockyer, have mixed feelings about the changes—perceiving that shortening the voting process can have a detrimental effect on the outcome by reducing the ability of voters to gain information during the primary voting process. Well-known and wealthy candidates may have an advantage. As William Schneider notes (1997, 734): "The 1996 contest also revealed the downside of front-loading. Candidates had to raise a lot of money early. That favored more-established figures such as Dole. Front-loading kept potentially strong candidates from running. And made it impossible for late starters to get in the race. 'I think we've probably made a mistake by front-loading these primaries,' GOP strategist Roger J. Stone said after last year's New Hampshire primary. 'It meant that good men like Jack Kemp and Colin Powell and Dick Cheney didn't make this race because they thought it was either unwinnable or too difficult.'" Many others have expressed comparable views. Texas Republican Chairman Tom Pauken was quoted in the August 14, 1996, *Fort Worth Star Telegram:* "1976, [Ronald] Reagan would have been knocked out in New Hampshire, but because primaries were spread out, he had the opportunity to bounce back in North Carolina and win in Texas. And that almost won him the nomination against Gerald Ford." Rhodes Cook argues that, historically, front-loading clearly advantages better known candidates (1997, p. 1942): "It is no accident that the last two times that dark horses successfully challenged front-runners for the Democratic nomination were in the 1970s (George McGovern in 1972 and Jimmy Carter in 1976). In that era, the primary season started slowly, and little-known candidates had the time to raise money and momentum after doing well in the early rounds."

But 20 years later, the dynamics of presidential nomination contests are substantially different. Jim Nicholson, chairman of the Republican National Committee's Rules Committee, remarked about the 1996 contest, "As the primary results from one state shifted the strength of candidates within the field, voters in the states next on the schedule often did not have enough time to thoroughly assess the field of candidates; they didn't have the opportunity to make a well-informed decision." While some early empirical work found that voters do not become more informed in drawn-out primaries (see Keeter and Zukin 1983), more recent studies find contrary results, supportive of Nicholson's view (see Alvarez and Glasgow 1997; Bartels 1988; Paolino 1996; Popkin 1991). Sequential voting as in drawn-out presidential primaries is seen as an opportunity for voters to learn during the electoral process and for voters to make more informed decisions; front-loading prevents voters from having that opportunity.

The Hazards of Weather and Shoe Boxes

In late October 1997 the Denver area experienced what many saw as a disruptive and particularly unwelcome crisis, an early severe snowstorm that almost paralyzed the city. However, the Regional Transportation District (RTD) of Denver, Colorado, viewed the event differently. The snowstorm gave them an opportunity to run ads extolling the light rail service's benefits, ads that they hoped would influence voters who would be deciding on a sales tax increase to expand the service in an election officially scheduled for Tuesday, November 4, 1997. Yet unlike earlier elections, voters had been encouraged to use mail-in and early balloting, and a substantial number of voters made their choices before the storm. Consequently, the ads missed a third of the voters. The measure went down in defeat.

As in drawn-out presidential primaries, mail-in and early balloting can change the way information and campaigns affect electoral choices. Kelly (1997) quotes pollster Floyd Ciruli: "The way campaigns spend money, the amount of advertising, the events, they all change in strange and unpredictable ways when you're voting over several weeks. . . . We've invented a new election cycle in this state."[3] Consider the experience of a congressional candidate in Washington state in 1996:

Brian Baird knew he had blown the election two years ago when the cheerful old lady whose vote he was soliciting told the Democratic candidate for Congress that she had already voted—by absentee ballot.

"She said she kept a shoe box on her kitchen table, where she put everything she received about the candidates," recalled Baird, from Washington state's 3rd Congressional District. "When she was ready to vote, she would dig into her box and study the literature.

"I remember thinking two things when I hung up the phone: Bless her heart, she's doing her level best to make an informed choice. And I wasn't in her shoe box."[4]

Baird lost the election by 887 absentee ballots.

Baird's experience demonstrates how campaigns are developing into early and later contests and voter knowledge can vary across these contests. Some have criticized mail-in balloting for the effect it can have on how information is used by voters. Sammon observes:

"Curtis Gans, director of the Committee for the Study of the American Electorate, said . . . mail voting weeks before the election can prevent voters from making fully informed choices based on information unveiled during the final weeks of the campaign. "What about people who would vote for Ross Perot by a mail ballot only to find that after they mailed in their vote, Perot started accusing the government of attempting to sabotage his daughter's wedding?" Gans asked rhetorically.[5]

Moreover, skeptics argue that early uninformed voters may have a disproportionate influence on electoral outcomes. Romano (1998) reports that these analysts maintain that "early voting can give an unfair advantage to the well-known and the well-financed candidates who attract support from the marginally informed on the strength of name recognition."

In addition, the news media may complicate the effect of early voting, as Vetter summarizes.

One complaint of the Oregon election is that it was possible for the media to find out who had voted when the ballots had been turned in, call those people and ask them how they voted. The media could have essentially kept a running score of how people had voted. Mike Devlin, the news director of KATU-TV in Oregon said in the *National Journal* that the media could find out how people had voted. *"Given the methods of modern-day polling, we could figure out which candidate was winning or, in some cases, had already won,"* he said.[6] (emphasis added)

These commentators worry that in extensive mail-in and early balloting, early voters' choices may be based on information different from that available to later voters, and early voters may have a significant effect on later choices through horse-race reporting in the media.

Sequential Voting in U.S. Elections

Both the jockeying in scheduling presidential primaries and the worries of negative effects from mail-in and early balloting illustrate the unknowns that exist about the effect of sequence on voter choices and electoral outcomes. How much does it matter who votes first in presidential primaries, or whether the voting in these primaries is drawn-out or front-loaded? How much does it matter whether elections are held over a period of time by mail and through early balloting as compared to voting restricted to one day?

The debate over the effect of sequence in voting has a historical precedent in the history of federal elections. The first federal selection of presidential electors in 1789 was held on the same date, the first Wednesday in January. However, because of differences in when state legislatures met it seemed impossible for the election to be held on the same date in the future. For over four months, the Second Congress debated the setting of the federal election calendar.[7] The debate centered over whether the period of time the states would choose electors would be short or long. Those in favor of a long period envisioned that the time would be used by electors to reach a consensus, while others worried about intrigue. The decision was, as was typical for the new republic, a compromise: electors would be chosen within 34 days of the first Wednesday in December.

Yet, as McCormick comments, this resolution led to "interesting consequences." He observes (1982, 45): "By the time the last states voted, for example, either the results of the presidential election might already have been determined or—as in 1800—the whole election might hinge on the vote of the final slate." In fact the disproportionate influence of early states' voters was apparently quite dramatic; McCormick relates: "It was notorious that in 1840 hordes of voters, having cast ballots in their home states, crossed into neighboring states with later election days and voted a second time" (208).[8] Consequently, in 1845 Congress legislated a uniform federal election day for the selection of the electors.[9] The regular election day was extended to congressional elections in 1872.[10]

The U.S. Supreme Court recently reaffirmed the right of Congress to legislate a uniform election day. On December 2, 1997, the Court, in *Foster v. Love,* declared Louisiana's nonpartisan electoral system for members of Congress unconstitutional. In Louisiana, at a date prior to the federal election date, voters would choose over all candidates for Congress, regardless of party affiliation. If one candidate received over 50 percent of the vote, that candidate was declared the winner at that time. If no candidate received a majority, a second, runoff election was held between the two top vote receivers on the federal election date. But this rarely happened. In Louisiana over 80 percent of congressional incumbents secured victory in the first stage, making the second stage, scheduled for the federal election day, unnecessary.[11]

In *Foster v. Love,* the Court noted that the uniform election day was legislated by Congress to prevent problems that can arise if voting is sequential. In particular, Congress in 1871 was concerned that earlier voters might have a disproportionate influence on the outcome of the election and on later voter choices. Justice David Souter wrote in the majority opinion:

> Our judgment is buttressed by an appreciation of Congress's object "to remedy more than one evil arising from the election of members of Congress occurring at different times in the different States." *Ex parte Yarbrough,* 110 U.S. 651, 661 (1884). As the sponsor of the original bill put it, Congress was concerned both with the distortion of the voting process threatened when the results of an early federal election in one State can influence later voting in other States, and with the burden on citizens forced to turn out on two different election days to make final selections of federal officers in presidential election years: "Unless we do fix some time at which, as a rule, Representatives shall be elected, it will be in the power of each State to fix upon a different day, and we may have a canvass going on all over the Union at different times. It gives some States undue advantage. . . . I can remember, in 1840, when the news from Pennsylvania and other States that held their elections prior to the presidential election settled the presidential election as effectually as it was afterward done. . . . I agree . . . that Indiana, Ohio, and Pennsylvania, by voting in October, have an influence. But what I contend is that it is an undue advantage, that it is a wrong, and that it is a wrong also to the people of those States, that once in four years they shall be put to the trouble of having a double election." Cong. Globe, 42nd Cong., 2d Sess., 141 (1871) (remarks of Rep. Butler).

Hence, Justice Souter contends that Congress legislated a uniform election day partly because of concerns that sequential voting for the president or members of Congress would lead to different outcomes than simultaneous voting if states that vote earlier have a greater influence than other states.[12]

Some policymakers believe that the same reasoning applies to the presidential primary process; a virtual national primary will lead to candidates who are preferred by the majority of voters in all states rather than those preferred by early voters who may not be representative of the national population. Similarly, concerns about fraud, disproportionate influence, and the information levels of early voters are seen as reasons to restrict early and mail-in balloting.

Simultaneous versus Sequential Voting

The debates over the virtual national primary and early and mail-in balloting illustrate two contrasting views about the timing of voting in elections:

- Early voters in sequential voting such as in drawn-out primaries or early and mail-in balloting may have an undue influence on the electoral outcome, and this influence may be problematic if the early voters are not representative or do not have the same information as the voting population as a whole on election day.
- Sequential voting such as in drawn-out primaries (and possibly early and mail-in balloting) may allow later voters to make more informed decisions (and perhaps "better" decisions) than they would in simultaneous voting as in the virtual national primary or single-day elections when there is a large number of potential candidates and voters have incomplete and asymmetric information about the candidates, knowing mainly about a well-financed front-runner.

The first concern is the downside of sequential voting while the second is the downside of simultaneous voting. Are these significant concerns? If so, which is more serious? Does the advantage of possible information accumulation that might occur in sequential voting overcome the disadvantage of possible unequal influence caused by differences in the preferences and information in early versus late voters? This is essentially the dilemma noted by California state senator Lockyer and the critics of mail-in and early voting.

In this book, we address these two concerns. We present a theoretical and empirical comparison of simultaneous voting elections (as in a national primary or other elections held on the same day) with sequential voting (as in drawn-out sequential primaries and mail-in and early balloting).

Our analysis is distinctive in that we use both a formal model to develop our theoretical predictions and laboratory experiments to evaluate them. It almost goes without saying that this is not the standard approach to studying presidential primaries or voting behavior in large elections. While there are a number of notable examples of formal models that have been used to examine the presidential primary election process and the effect of sequence in elections in general, which we review in chapter 4 (e.g., see the models of Aldrich 1980a,b; Abramowitz and Stone 1984; Brady 1996; Cooper and Munger 1996; Dekel and Piccione 1997; Fey 1996; Strumpf 1997; Witt 1997), we know of no other experimental study of how sequential and simultaneous voting work in presidential primaries and other elections combined with a formal model.

We use a formal model because of the advantages that it provides. Specifically, by formally stating the assumptions that we make about voters, voter choice processes, sequential voting elections, and simultaneous voting elections, we can derive predictions that are logically consistent with these assumptions. Empirical evaluation of predictions from theories with clearly stated assumptions can provide greater insight into the value of the theoretical formulation—our view of the electoral process—and whether this view is empirically supported. Because we wish this book to be accessible to many readers who may not be familiar with the workings of formal voting models such as ours, we review the literature on formal voting models in chapter 4, and in appendix A we discuss the basics of formal models more extensively. In the presentation of our theory in chapter 5, we attempt to provide simple and clear explanations whenever possible.

We also believe that an experimental approach has unique advantages, which we also address in appendix A. In general, we turn to experiments for two primary reasons. First, experiments have advantages in evaluating formal models because of the control that they allow the researcher to maintain through the experimental design. In our experiments, we can control variables that might be difficult, if not impossible, to measure or manipulate in the naturally occurring environment. Second, because of the small number of contests where presidential primaries have dominated the selection process of presidential nominees (only since 1972) and the relatively recent and still limited use of early and mail-in balloting procedures, there is little naturally occurring data that can answer the theoretical questions we pose. Moreover, real-world experimenting with new electoral procedures (allowing voters to choose in sequence, for example) is potentially far more costly than in the laboratory. In the laboratory our subjects make "real" choices that have "real" consequences—their payments depend on the votes they make, as we describe in chapter 6—but the real consequences are less than the election of candidates that may not be preferable for society when we experiment with electoral procedures in naturally occurring elections. We believe that the experimental approach has a unique advantage in building understanding of how different electoral systems work that can be useful for policymakers in the future.

Plan of the Book

In the next two chapters, we discuss the history and problems of voting order in U.S. elections. In chapter 2, we explore the evolution of the current presidential primary election process and the issues of front-loading and representativeness more extensively. We illustrate how front-loading has led to a virtual national primary and the reasons for concerns about the representativeness of early primary voters in drawn-out primaries. We discuss mail-in and early balloting in chapter 3. We examine the reasons for and against allowing this type of sequential voting and the existing empirical evidence on the effects of such systems on voting behavior and electoral outcomes.

Chapter 4 summarizes the formal theoretical literature on presidential primaries and sequential voting in general. We argue that, while insightful, the existing theoretical work cannot address the fundamental comparison of the virtual national primary with sequential drawn-out primaries or the concerns about early and mail-in balloting. Chapter 5 presents our basic voting model and theoretical predictions. Chapter 6 explains our experimental design and describes the results of our experimental analysis of simultaneous voting as compared with sequential voting. In chapter 7, we examine the effect of representativeness in sequential voting. Chapter 8 reflects upon our results and the implications for future research on the presidential primary process and other sequential voting systems like mail-in and early balloting. In addition to an explanation of formal models and the role of experiments, the appendixes contain technical details of our formal model and proofs of the theoretical predictions, a copy of the instructions and quiz used in the sequential voting experiments, and particulars on the empirical results presented in chapters 7 and 8.

CHAPTER 2

The Evolution of Front-Loading and the Importance of Primary Status

On December 2, 1913, newly elected president Woodrow Wilson gave his first State of the Union address to a joint session of the U.S. Congress. He spoke of the difficulties of dealing with the current Mexican government, the lack of available financial credit for farmers, and other matters bearing on the nation. But he also advocated a serious change in the nation's electoral system.

> I turn to a subject which I hope can be handled promptly and without serious controversy of any kind. I mean the method of selecting nominees for the Presidency of the United States. I feel confident that I do not misinterpret the wishes or the expectations of the country when I urge the prompt enactment of legislation which will provide for primary elections throughout the country at which the voters of the several parties may choose their nominees for the Presidency without the intervention of nominating conventions. (1966, 2548)

Yet, Wilson's proposed national presidential primary legislation remained unpassed. Nevertheless, over 80 years later presidential primaries do dominate nominations, and some argue that they are evolving into a virtual national primary through front-loading, giving Wilson his wish. How has this happened? And what do we know about the process of presidential nominee selection today? In this chapter, we explore the history of the presidential nomination process and the developments of characteristics of current presidential primaries. We believe that understanding this history helps us better comprehend the complicated nature of the present system.

When Conventions Made Real Choices

The World before Primaries

The history of early presidential electoral politics is intricately connected to the story of the development of the American party system; it is excellently reviewed elsewhere (see, e.g., Aldrich 1993; Epstein 1986; McCormick 1982). Here we highlight the ways in which parties' processes of nominating candidates for the presidency evolved into the present front-loaded system and the concerns of policymakers that resulted.

Initially the early U.S. parties worked through caucuses composed of party members serving in Congress to choose nominees for president. However, as the mass political party developed, it became clear that these choices were not electable and were affected by the limited membership of the caucus. Parties gradually turned to national conventions, drawing delegates from state parties, which had developed over time along national party divisions. By the 1840s, national mass electoral parties, really confederations of the state parties, had evolved, and the process of choosing nominees for the presidency by national conventions of delegates from the state parties had taken hold. The important impact of this period for our current system is that it established the role of parties as more than legislative caucuses—and cemented the role of states and individual voters, at first indirectly, in the presidential nomination process.

Primaries in a Supporting Role

The Advent of Presidential Primaries

The advent of presidential primaries in 1901 changed the process of presidential nominations although party leaders still retained ultimate control over nominations until after 1968. Direct primaries were an innovation of the Progressive movement and were used widely by the turn of the century for nominations for statewide office. As Jewell explains, direct primaries served different purposes in Northern and Southern states. In the West and Midwest direct primaries were attractive for two reasons: "a theoretical belief in direct democracy" and "because the primary offered the best vehicle for wresting control over the parties—and nominations—from conservative forces. The Progressives concentrated most of their efforts on the Republican party, which was the normal majority party in most states. The Democratic party usually offered a poor alternative, both because of voter loyalties to the Republican party and because Democratic leadership was often conservative and/or ineffective" (1984, 7).

The South, in contrast, used direct primaries with participation restricted to whites in order to maintain white Democratic control over the region as discussed in Kousser 1974. The conservative Southern Democratic leadership feared that factions within the party might break away and mobilize black voters. They established the norm that unsuccessful white candidates would not challenge the nominees in general elections. Since blacks were largely Republican and other measures had restricted black voter turnout, such as poll taxes and literacy tests, the direct primary allowed the white Democratic party to maintain control by handling dissent within its ranks.

Direct primaries were first extended to presidential nominations in 1901 when Florida passed a law allowing state parties to conduct direct primaries to select national convention delegates.[1] When the national Republican party rebuffed Governor Robert La Follette's delegates for others chosen in caucuses controlled by party elites in 1904, Wisconsin enacted direct primaries for presidential nominations the following year. The early use of presidential primaries was motivated by the natural desires of the new state leaders either to secure dominion from old state party leadership as in Wisconsin or to maintain white Democratic domination in the South. Presidential primaries were then much more prevalent in Northern states than Southern ones, however. The first modern presidential primary law that resembles the ones used now was enacted in Oregon in 1910 where voters selected between both competing candidates and delegate slates. By 1912 California, Illinois, Indiana, Massachusetts, Nebraska, New Jersey, New York, Pennsylvania, and South Dakota had instituted presidential primaries. In his attempt to take over the Republican party in 1912, Theodore Roosevelt competed in these presidential primaries, winning nine. However, he was unsuccessful at the convention because of the dominance of Taft supporters among the delegates.[2]

The idea of presidential primaries replacing state conventions was definitely popular among some policymakers and academics. In 1915, Dickey called for national presidential primaries in the *American Political Science Review*. We noted above that Woodrow Wilson, in his First Annual Message after election, also advocated expanding the role of primaries. Nonetheless, Wilson's desired legislation was not enacted and, in fact, only states have explicit regulation of candidate nomination procedures of parties; there is no regulation of nominations at the federal level.[3]

The Decline of Primaries

Despite continued growth in presidential primaries (reaching a peak in 1916 with 20 Republican primaries accounting for 58.9 percent of delegates), they declined in use in the 1920s.[4] As Palmer remarks, presidential primaries "had not produced candidates with mass popular appeal and had proved time-consuming and often prohibitively expensive. The prospect of unwanted nominees foisted by ignorant voters on reluctant party leaders dimmed its luster still further, while to most party officials the primary represented an open invitation to fratricidal conflict" (1997, 68).

It is interesting that while some states eliminated primaries, others used methods of restricting choices so that primaries could still be used for statewide offices but had less of an effect on presidential nominations. Ceasar summarizes that some states retrenched from Progressive reforms by "the de facto insulation of the primaries from the national focus through laws that barred delegates from specifying on the ballot which candidate they preferred; and the development of a tradition in some states, enforced by the power of the state parties, of running favorite sons in the primaries" (1982, 24). Many existing presidential primaries never had specifications on the ballot for the presidential candidates but only listed the delegates.[5]

It appears then that the motivations behind the use of primaries for statewide offices in the late nineteenth and early twentieth centuries did not translate well to the presidency. That is, while primaries had been used in the South to prevent white factions of the Democratic party from breaking out and joining with black Republican voters within the states, this was less an issue in presidential nomination contests in these states where state-level races were sufficient for the unification desired.[6] Presidential primaries, even during the heydey of the Progressives, were used on a much more limited basis in the South. As Progressives decreased in strength in Republican states, their ability to wrest control, never sufficiently strong at the national level, diminished. Thus, presidential primaries declined.

Making Primaries Count and Premonitions of Front-Loading
Nevertheless primaries did continue to play a role in presidential nominations, and that role increased over time. Palmer reports that in 1928 Al Smith and Herbert Hoover used primaries, in one case to demonstrate that a Catholic could receive votes outside New York and in the other to squash a possible opponent. In 1932, Franklin D. Roosevelt attempted to use primaries to discourage Smith. Wendell Willkie's lack of success in Wisconsin's 1944 primary hurt his chances for selection as the Republican nominee. Most notably Harold Stassen, from Minnesota, in 1948 came close to using primary victories combined with media publicity to take an underdog route to nomination.

Stassen's success induced midwestern states such as Indiana, Montana, and Minnesota to revive their presidential primaries by 1952. Palmer argues that not just the increase in primaries but the candidacy of Eisenhower marked "a pivotal year in the emergence of the modern campaign process." He notes, "The candidacy of General Eisenhower was launched by the New Hampshire primary of March 1952. In this and succeeding primaries, the general's backers demonstrated their candidate's popular appeal to national and state Republican party leaders and to the electorate at large. Eisenhower's victories proved crucial for delegate accumulation and in wresting the nomination from Robert Taft at the convention" (1997, 69).

But Eisenhower was not the only successful candidate influenced by presidential primary victories after World War II. Adlai Stevenson, despite receiving the Democratic nomination in 1952 without participation in primaries, attained the nomination in 1956 after defeating Estes Kefauver in the California primary. As with Willkie in 1944, he entered primaries to demonstrate that he could win despite losing as his party's nominee in the previous presidential election. In 1960, John F. Kennedy used primaries to demonstrate his electability to Democratic party leaders. Richard M. Nixon was a primary winner in Republican primaries both in 1960 and 1968. Barry Goldwater used success in primaries to achieve the Republican nomination in 1964. The first rejection of a primary winner since 1956, that of Eugene McCarthy in 1968, was, as Epstein states, "in extraordinary and politically disastrous circumstances."

More telling than the relationship between primary winners and nomination choices from 1956 on is the fact that from 1948 for Republicans and 1952 for Democrats nominations were decided on the first convention ballot. Party leaders increasingly appeared to make commitments prior to conventions. Conventions were becoming less significant in determining the nominee, that is, the negotiation and bargaining were occurring *before* the convention and *whether by primary victories or high standings in polls, nominees were expected to demonstrate that they had public support.* The nomination determination was occurring earlier in the electoral season and was influenced by primaries. State party leaders began to make commitments and negotiate earlier, a premonition of front-loading.

States and Parties

During the mixed period, there were also other changes whose effects on the national parties' presidential nomination process became more obvious post-1968. Along with direct primaries, other electoral reforms were enacted by the Progressives such as adoption of the secret ballot. By regulating ballot access and adopting primaries for statewide offices, states began to regulate how state and local parties selected their nominees for office. Whether parties could use conventions or primaries, whether the primaries were open or closed to non–party members, and requirements that designated party membership were regulated. Yet, no regulation of these processes developed at the national level at this time. Moreover, as voting rights cases challenged the white primary in the South, Southern states attempted to deregulate parties vesting significant power in the individual parties, which they then argued were not constitutionally subject to the same voting rights laws.[7] Thus, states adopted myriad complicated and distinct processes for regulation of the state parties, which made up the national confederated parties. These regulations continue to vex and complicate national party decisions—for example, California recently changed its electoral law to allow for blanket primaries, a type of open primaries, which is contrary to national party rules for presidential primaries.[8]

These regulations can affect the types of candidates parties nominate. Gerber and Morton (1998), examining congressional voting patterns from 1982 to 1990, demonstrate that when congressional members are chosen via closed primaries they are more extreme ideologically relative to voters in their districts than those chosen via closed primaries where new and/or independent voters are allowed to vote or open ones where all voters can participate. Thus, these regulatory choices at the state level can significantly affect parties' nominations. During the mixed period, these regulations did not substantially matter to the national parties since primaries did not dominate the presidential nomination process. For example, Wisconsin's use of an open primary law for presidential nominations was unchallenged by the national party until primaries became determinant post-1968.[9]

A second development during the mixed period that has had more of an effect post-1968 is the beginning of a centralization and expansion of the staff of the national organization during the post–World War II period, as detailed in Epstein 1986. As Shafer 1983 documents, the reforms post-1968 were largely developed by the Democratic national commission and staff with little influence from the confederation of state parties. But while nationalization began in party organizations, the regulation of parties continued to be principally a state-level function.

Impacts of the Mixed System

We believe that the current dilemmas in presidential primary contests are partly a consequence of the developments during the mixed period. Three such developments are important.

- Parties, their nomination processes, and elections in general are largely regulated at the state level. This makes any kind of national reform of the presidential nomination process difficult. It is one of the reasons why front-loading has occurred—states may all prefer that contests be spread apart, but because they see that their own self-interest is served by moving closer to the front of the season, primaries end up bunched together.
- Conventions largely ceased to be the place where nominations were settled—gradually candidates were nominated on first ballots. This meant that delegates were becoming "promised" prior to conventions and that the process by which delegates became promised became more important to securing nomination.
- National political parties arose, with formal staffs and goals. However, the relationship between the national parties and candidates became complex since national rules can have effects on which candidates are selected.

Primaries in a Starring Role

Reforms That Mattered

Much has been written about the post-1968 Democratic reforms in delegate selection and the consequences these reforms have had for the presidential nomination process (see in particular Abramowitz and Stone 1984; Aldrich 1980a, 1993; Ceasar 1982; Epstein 1986; Keeter and Zukin 1983; Polsby 1983; Shafer 1983). In general, the post-1968 period has led to the dominance of primaries in determining presidential nominees. Other changes during the post-1968 period, of course, had a contributing influence on presidential campaigns such as campaign finance legislation and the increasing power of the national news media. Certainly the constraints on campaigns financed through federal matching funds has been a concern and is likely to affect the 2000 race strongly. But the arrival of national rules controlling how state parties selected delegates has had a profound effect. Interestingly, although only the Democrats officially reformed their presidential nomination system, the Republican party was also significantly affected, primarily because of the necessity for coordination of state regulation over both parties.

The changes in the rules post-1968 are rather complicated and have been manipulated over time. The principal original goal of these reforms was to open up the process by which non-primary states chose delegates to a broader spectrum of party members. Palmer (1997, 70–75) and Keefe (1998, 91–108) summarize the changes and variations in national party primary rules from 1968 to 1996.

The major constant across the rule changes is the requirement for participation of rank-and-file party members either through direct primaries or restrictions on caucus-convention choice systems. Yet, the variations that have occurred over time are instructive. First, while there is a definite preference throughout the 30 years for delegate choice in the Democratic party to be proportional to vote totals, there are also consequential deviations over time in the degree of proportional representation and the tendency to reintroduce a role for party leaders. The first reform commission (McGovern-Fraser, 1969–72) eliminated the unit rule and required that at least 75 percent of each state delegation be selected at a level no higher than congressional districts. The Mikulski Commission (1972–73) required proportional representation with a few exceptions, forcing California for example to change from winner-take-all to proportional representation. Candidates were required, however, to meet a 10 percent threshold that was later increased to 15 percent. The Winograd Commission (1975–78) permitted states with at-large delegates to set their own thresholds, with a 25 percent threshold for delegates chosen at the district level, but banned winner-take-all primaries for the 1980 election. The Hunt Commission (1981–82) allowed some states to have winner-take-all primaries, "winner-take-more" where winners got extra delegates, and created "superdelegates" (14 percent) for the 1984 convention that were chosen on the basis of party status or public office. The Fairness Commission (1984–85) increased the number of super-delegates for the 1988 convention but lowered the threshold to 15 percent. In 1992, winner-take-all and winner-take-more primaries were banned yet again. Palmer notes:

> The DNC's prevarication over this issue was symptomatic of the vulner-ability of successive rules reviews to the whims of powerful candidates such as Carter, Mondale, and Jesse Jackson. It also demonstrated the im-portance that delegate allocation was deemed to have in determining the dynamics of primary momentum. Proportionate allocation, the commis-sion believed, would take the edge off Iowa and New Hampshire by slow-ing the pace of delegate accumulation and forcing candidates to spread their resources more evenly. The presence of winner-take-all primaries later in the contest was, conversely, seen as essential in persuading candi-dates not to fold their tents after discouraging early results. (1997, 75)

While the Democratic party has gone back and forth over whether to al-low winner-take-all primaries, Republicans, on the other hand, have been ag-nostic on the issue and, as a consequence, more Republican primaries are win-ner-take-all. Moreover, Republicans allow for open primary participation of non–party members if a state chooses, while the Democratic party again has ei-ther banned outright or allowed only a few open primaries. Thus, while both Democratic and Republican primaries have become dominant in determining the nominees of these parties and are subject to many of the same state regula-tions, there are important party differences in the way presidential primaries are held. Winner-take-all elections can allow a candidate to gain large delegate counts more quickly, leading to shorter contests. Furthermore, as noted above, Gerber and Morton (1998) find evidence that in states with more open primaries members of Congress are more moderate relative to the voters in their districts, suggesting that presidential nominees may be affected by the difference.

Primaries Rise Again

As mentioned in the previous section, the writing of the first set of reforms was largely dominated by members of the Democratic national commission and staff. Ironically, the reformers believed that by making state and local caucuses more open, there would be a decline in demand for presidential primaries and that primaries might actually decrease in use and influence with a rise in cau-cus use. Instead many states opted to add direct primaries.

This has occurred for a number of reasons. First, the caucus process under the new rules is more complicated to manage, with required participation first at the precinct level, then a county convention culminating in a statewide convention. The detailed requirements added the specter of having a state's delegation refused a role at the convention as Richard Daley's 1972 Illinois delegation. Second, there is an advantage to states from the media exposure of a primary election. Finally, state party leaders may fear that ideological extremists, or supporters of particular candidates, will dominate caucus choices leading to candidates that will be less successful with the general public. There is evidence that caucus participants are more unrepresentative of the general electorate than primary voters; in particular they are stronger partisans and more ideological (see Greer 1988; Hagen 1989; Norrander 1989; Stone, Abramowitz, and Rapoport 1989). While Abramowitz and Stone (1983) find evidence that party activists are concerned with matters of electability, Norrander (1993) finds that the candidate choices in presidential caucus states are more ideologically extreme than those in states that use presidential primaries.

The increase in the use of presidential primaries after 1968 is startling given that prior to 1968 the last increase in presidential primaries had occurred in 1956 when Florida Republicans and the District of Columbia first held primaries. Table 2.1 summarizes the number of states using presidential primaries in the period 1968 through 2000 and the percentage of delegates selected by primaries. In 1968, only 16 states and the District of Columbia had presidential primaries (Alabama, California, Florida, Illinois, Indiana, Massachusetts, Nebraska, New Hampshire, New Jersey, New York, Ohio, Oregon, Pennsylvania, South Dakota, West Virginia, and Wisconsin). By 1972, six more states switched to presidential primaries: Maryland, Michigan, New Mexico, North Carolina, Rhode Island, and Tennessee. By 1976 seven more states switched: Georgia, Idaho, Kentucky, Montana, Nevada, Texas, and Vermont; while only New Mexico switched back to a caucus-convention system. Arkansas made its optional primary compulsory. In less than 10 years, the number of states holding presidential primaries had almost doubled.

This trend continued into 1980 when 35 states and other convention constituencies in the Democratic party and 34 in the Republican party used presidential primaries. However, 1984 did experience a decline as a number of states dropped their primaries, and only 25 Democratic and 30 Republican states and other convention constituencies held presidential primaries. Yet, these numbers rebounded by 1988 almost to previous levels. Since 1988, the number of Democratic primaries has leveled off while the number of Republican primaries has continued to increase substantially. In 2000, 38 states held Democratic presidential primaries, and 40 held Republican presidential primaries.

The number of delegates selected by presidential primaries rather than caucus-conventions experienced a similar strong increase. In 1968, 37.5 and

TABLE 2.1.   Presidential Primaries, 1968–2000

	Democratic		Republican	
Year	Number of States	Percentage of Delegate Votes	Number of States	Percentage of Delegate Votes
1968	17	37.5	16	34.3
1972	23	60.5	22	52.7
1976	29	72.6	28	67.9
1980	35	71.8	34	76.0
1984	25	62.1	30	71.0
1988	34	66.6	35	76.0
1992	36	69.6	39	79.1
1996	36	62.8	43	88.3
2000	38	87.4	40	88.5

34.3 percent of Democratic and Republican delegates were chosen by presidential primaries. By 1976, these percentages were 72.6 and 67.9 percent and in 1980, 71.8 and 76 percent. The percentage of Democratic delegates selected by primaries has declined slightly but stayed generally above 60 percent reflecting the use of superdelegates. It is striking to note that although the reforms were written and devised to change the Democratic party, they had a somewhat larger effect on the way Republican party delegates are chosen in that, by 2000, 88.5 percent of Republican delegates were selected through presidential primaries. This is partly because both parties are affected by changes in state regulations to satisfy the national Democratic party requirements.

Nevertheless, Republicans have continued to use some methods by which voter preferences and delegate selection are disconnected. Some states formerly had a legal ban on the identification of a delegate's presidential candidate. While the Democratic national party had achieved full compliance with a prohibition on this type of primary by 1976, Republican primaries in Illinois, Mississippi, New York, and Pennsylvania used this type of primary in 1980. Republicans have not attempted to reduce winner-take-all primaries. In 2000 over half of the Republican primaries were winner-take-all; some used winner-take-all if a candidate received a majority of the vote, proportional representation if not; and about a fourth used proportional representation. Thus Republican contests benefit early front-runners more than Democratic ones do.

The two national parties also differ significantly in which voters are allowed to participate in the delegate selection process. While the Democratic party has attempted to restrict participation in primaries and caucuses to party members (requiring with some few exceptions closed primaries or caucuses), the Republican party has allowed open primaries and caucuses, allowing for crossover voting by non–party members. Moreover, Republicans do not have superdelegates like Democrats. Thus, Democratic controls suggest that delegates are chosen by a more representative group of rank-and-file party members and party elites, while Republican controls allow for delegates to be chosen by a wider distribution of the general electorate.

Spaced-Out Primaries: 1972–84

While the increase in primaries is the most notable aspect of the plebiscitary system, there are differences that have occurred during the period that are substantial. Basically, two types of plebiscitary candidate nominations have occurred: nomination contests where voting is sequential and drawn-out and nomination contests where voting is closer to simultaneous as in a virtual national primary because of front-loading. The first contests under the new system (1972, 1976, 1980) are clearly more drawn-out than the later ones (1988, 1992, 1996), with 1984's contest a mixture. In the first contests, it became apparent that the schedule of primaries mattered; this realization led to manipulation of the schedule and front-loading. We examine why sequence mattered under the plebiscitary period more than under the mixed period and the issue of representativeness of early primaries in this section. In the next section, we examine the extent of front-loading.

When Sequence Did Not Matter

In the later years of the mixed period, while demonstrating public support either through polls or primaries was crucial for securing the presidential nomination of the major parties and evidence exists that much of the bargaining occurred prior to the national convention, the sequence and schedule of primaries was not as big an issue as it was to become post-1968. The proliferation of primaries made the sequence in which they were scheduled important. Prior to 1972, since primaries did not determine the outcome, candidates could pick and choose which primaries to enter and seek support from convention delegates based on poll results as well as primary outcomes. The key is that during the mixed period candidates for the nomination entered primaries to gain votes at the convention (achieve direct popular support, which gained a set of delegates) but also used polls and other mechanisms to influence state party leaders (who determined the vast majority of the delegates). Polls and other mechanisms could play an important role pre-1972, and the sequence of the primary outcomes was less important.

Post-1968, primary delegate votes are a greater percentage of the outcome. But the mechanics of caucus-convention choices are also significantly different because rank-and-file members were given greater roles in determining delegate choices. With greater participation by rank-and-file party members both through direct primaries and in caucus-conventions, the majority of delegate votes now were in the hands of these members rather than party leaders. The sequence in which rank-and-file members across the nation made their choices became important in determining the outcome.

Why Sequence Became Important

"Big Mo"

In order to understand how the change affected the role of sequence in primary elections we must explore how the dynamics of the plebiscitary system works. At a macro level, Aldrich (1980a,b) and Bartels (1988) examine how candidates in the new system who invest resources early in the presidential primary season increase the probability of selection in early primaries, which generates increased resources and media coverage, which then increases the probability of success in later primaries giving candidates momentum (or decay). Candidates recognize the influence of momentum—Bartels (1988, 27) discusses candidate George Bush's labeling of it as "Big Mo" in 1980 after his success in Iowa's caucuses that year. Clearly post-1968 candidates are entering races sooner, visiting states earlier, and attempting to build a solid campaign base as Palmer 1997 discusses (76–77).[10]

Micro-level Explanations of Momentum

But what is the micro model of voters that underlies these dynamics at the macro level? Early research on presidential election campaigns in the 1940s suggested that voters do not alter their preferences much during the campaigns, concluding that campaigns and the mass media had a minimal effect on voter preferences. Moreover, in an early study of voter information levels during the 1980 primary season, Keeter and Zukin (1983) argue that there is little evidence that voters "learn" during the electoral process. Thus, preliminary work would suggest that at the micro level the campaign should not affect voters substantially.

However, recent research on the post-1968 period shows a different story. Bartels (1988) and Popkin (1991) demonstrate that during presidential primary campaigns voter information levels do change in response to campaign events and news media reports. Popkin asserts that voters with weak to no preferences among the candidates, except perhaps a dislike for the front-runner, use information from the early primaries to judge which alternative candidate is the most viable. Kenney and Rice (1994) consider psychological theories of voter choices that might lead to macro-level momentum, and Norrander (1993) shows how candidate preferences of voters developed during the 1988 contest. Paolino (1998) considers momentum as a function of both voter perceptions of viability and certainty in those perceptions.

Relevant to the approach taken in this research, Alvarez and Glasgow (1997) consider a Bayesian model of voter learning, which they apply to the 1976 and 1980 primary election campaigns. The Bayesian model assumes that voters have prior views about candidate positions on issues. As voters acquire new information, they update these priors, forming posterior evaluations of candidates. It is an application of an expected utility model of voting choices when voters have imperfect information. In expected utility models, voters are assumed to consider in making decisions both their utility or satisfaction from each possible event or outcome and the probability that the outcome can occur.[11] In our model, we also assume that voters use Bayesian updating when they acquire new information about candidates.[12]

Alvarez and Glasgow argue that the effect of new information on voter choices depends on the certainty of voters' previous information and their own policy preferences. They point out the importance of early information.

> Early in a presidential primary, when voter knowledge of the positions of the candidates is very uncertain, new information, even if it is also uncertain, can produce large changes in the voter's perceptions of the candidate's position, their uncertainty of that position, *and even in their preferences*. This provides a theoretical account for the volatility witnessed early in the primary season in voter preferences and perceptions. They have imprecise knowledge, and learning new information in an uncertain situation can have dramatic consequences.

> So generally, we expect information to have different effects across the course of a presidential campaign. Early in the primary season, when knowledge is imprecise, a little new information can go a long way—even as far as changing a voter's preferences. But late in the general election, in the weeks before the general election, voters will typically have precise priors about the positions of the candidates. So even a lot of new information, even precise new information, will not induce a change in voter preferences. Late in the campaign, though, the major sources of change should instead be in the precision of their beliefs; that is, in their certainty about the issue positions of candidates. (1997, 11)

Voters, then, by gaining new information, can discover that their preferences over the candidates in terms of how they would vote may change during the campaign. The assumption of the Bayesian updating model is that voters' underlying preferences over the type of candidate they most prefer are not changing, but that their opinions of how candidates match their ideal choices are changing with new information.

Alvarez and Glasgow (1997), using data on both media reports and voter evaluations, find support for their Bayesian model in the 1976 and 1980 primaries. Interestingly, they show that in 1976 voters demonstrate a high level of learning about Carter, when he began as an unknown, and much less in 1980 when he ran as an incumbent, despite the fact that in both cases the amount of substantive information provided about Carter during the campaign was large. Similarly, examining 1984, Bartels (1988) finds that at the beginning of the campaign, voter evaluations of Mondale are initially more well formed (i.e., based on Mondale and his campaign positions) than those of Hart (which were based more on anti-Mondale sentiment), but during the course of the campaign, the evaluations of Hart became more like the evaluations of other candidates (based on Hart and his campaign positions).

Macro and Micro Combined

These studies of voter information suggest that the macro dynamic analyses, which emphasize the importance of early primary results, can be explained by the consequences of early primaries on voter information levels. Information flows occurred during the primary seasons in 1976, 1980, and 1984, and voters appeared to update their evaluations of candidates based on this information. These updates, if they revealed that a candidate's positions were significantly different than a voter's prior view, could result in voter preference changes. This is *more* likely to happen for candidates who are unknown at the start of the electoral campaign than for candidates who are well known or for all candidates later in the electoral campaign. Thus early primaries matter when primaries are drawn-out in that they *can* affect the information that voters have about the candidates and may have *significant* effects (when candidates are relatively unknown) on voter preferences.

In chapter 5 we argue that the types of information that voters have during the primary process include both substantive and horse-race information. One of our foci is on how voters use horse-race reports to infer substantive information. For our purposes in this chapter we only emphasize that there is clearly empirical evidence that voters learn during the primary season, and this is why early primaries, post-1968, became much more important in the nomination race. As momentum became important, who started the momentum also became important.

The Dominance of the Backward

Once it became clear that early primaries played a significant role in the dynamics of nomination campaigns, early primary states became subject to considerable criticism as nonrepresentative. Generally, New Hampshire has been the subject of the most criticism. Palmer 1997, chapter 2, discusses the types of criticisms and the reasonableness of these in considerable detail. Clearly some have oversimplified New Hampshire as Polsby discusses when he describes the then-current complaints about the primary process: "Complaints have largely been made about excessive expenditures of money, time, and energy, about a process that stretches out too long, about how the early primaries totally dominate the process and obliterate the significance of later ones in spite of the incapacity of any small cluster of states to 'represent' all the rest, never mind tiny New Hampshire with its elderly population, its large French-speaking minority, its backward economy, and its lack of state-wide communication other than the wildly idiosyncratic *Manchester Union-Leader*" (1983, 173).

While these criticisms are extreme and (Palmer argues) a bit unfair, there is evidence that New Hampshire is ideologically different from many states. One important aspect of New Hampshire politics is that the state's two parties are highly polarized. Erikson, Wright, and McIver (1993) measure the degree of polarization between the two major political parties in states and find that New Hampshire's is the sixth highest in the nation, suggesting that in both parties the average party member is more extreme than the average party member in most other states. Keeter and Zukin 1983 also conclude that New Hampshire Democrats are more liberal and Republicans more conservative than national party members.

New Hampshire is also greatly Republican. Erikson, Wright, and McIver (1993, 55) measure the effect of living in New Hampshire versus living in Arkansas (highly Democratic): "The difference in party identification produced by the difference between the political cultures of Arkansas and New Hampshire (40.8 points) approaches the partisan consequence of being Jewish instead of Protestant (55.9) or of being black instead of white (59.4)! And remember that the state coefficients are derived from an analysis in which all major demographic variables are controlled. These differences in state effects on partisanship are *not* a function of the measured state demographics."

Thus, if it is true that New Hampshire voters, through their choices, affect the outcome of the presidential nomination process by affecting the dynamics of the electoral campaign, then the ideological nonrepresentativeness of the state may be important. This is, of course, one of the things that we examine later in our theoretical and empirical study. The point here is that empirical evidence from the primary seasons of 1976, 1980, and 1984 suggests that voters gain information, which affects their choices as primaries progress. That gain appears to have occurred in response to outcomes in early primaries where voters may be very nonrepresentative of the rest of the electorate. When primaries are drawn-out—sequential—then voters gain information during the primary process, but that information can be colored by the nonrepresentativeness of the early voters.

Front-Loaded Primaries: 1988–2000

As discussed above, the first presidential elections of the plebiscitary period had generally drawn-out primaries, which caused many to be concerned about the influence of nonrepresentative early voters on the candidate nomination process. This is one cause for the substantial front-loading of the primary process that has occurred since 1984. Figures 2.1 and 2.2 show how the percentage of primaries completed by week in the primary season has risen over time. Figures 2.3 and 2.4 show how the percentage of delegates selected by primaries by week of the primary season has changed with election year.

In chapter 1 and above, we emphasize the "fear of undue influence" cause for front-loading. However, there is ample evidence that, when they are able, candidates have attempted to manipulate the scheduling of primaries to their advantage. Drawn-out primaries are more likely to benefit less well-known candidates since voters' information about these candidates is more likely to be increased and voter preferences may be more affected, as found by Alvarez and Glasgow (1997) and Bartels (1988). Thus, front-runners who may be well-known gain less from drawn-out primaries than do unknown candidates. Front-runners recognize this benefit and have historically attempted to influence the primary process.

As Palmer remarks: "With the formation of the Winograd Commission in 1976, primary scheduling became a target for candidate organizations seeking to mold the timetable to their political advantage, and post-Mikulski reform bodies soon degenerated into intraparty squabbles between the most influential candidates of the period" (1997, 78). Democratic national reforms have generally led to a shorter primary season. The Winograd Commission shortened the Democratic primary season from six to three months, while the Hunt Commission reduced the period of time between the Iowa caucuses and the New Hampshire primary from 36 days to eight.[13] In contrast, until 1996, the Republican national party had not attempted to control the primary schedule.[14]

Perhaps the first example of front-loading was not the movement of a primary to an earlier date, but the movement of Iowa's caucuses in 1972 ahead of New Hampshire's historical first-in-the-nation primary. Iowa's caucuses became an important early stomping ground for candidates, and publicity followed.[15] Front-loading began in earnest with the first Southern regional primary, labeled Super Tuesday, held on the second Tuesday in March 1984. While the first Super Tuesday involved a total of nine states (five primaries and four caucus-conventions held simultaneously), in 1988 21 states and convention regions held primaries or caucuses on one Super Tuesday date resulting in the selection of 31.4 percent of Democratic delegates and 33.1 percent of Republican delegates simultaneously.[16]

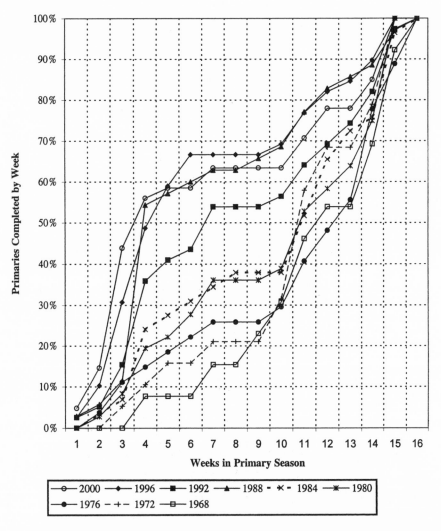

Fig. 2.1. Republican primary compression

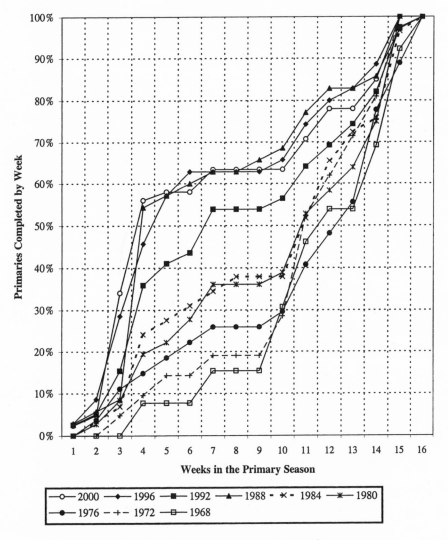

Fig. 2.2. Democratic primary compression

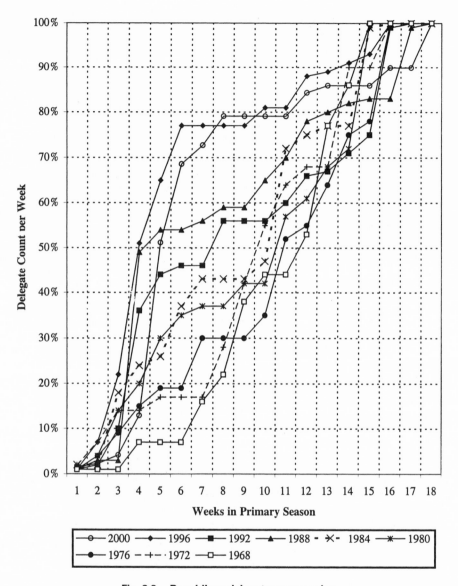

Fig. 2.3. Republican delegate compression

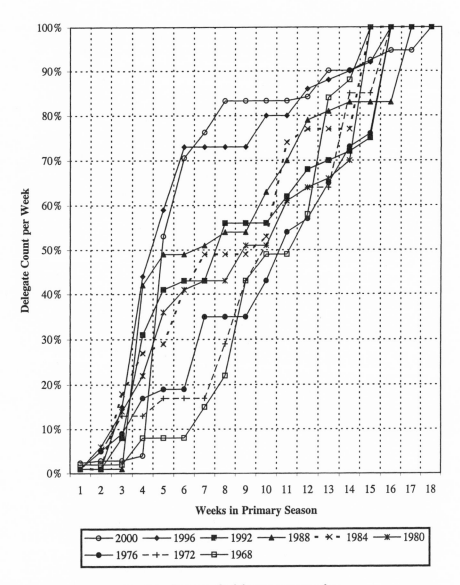

Fig. 2.4. Democratic delegate compression

The effect of front-loading in 1988 was felt by the candidates significantly in that it hurt their ability to capitalize on success in Iowa and New Hampshire. Wilcox compares 1984 and 1988: "In 1984, Gary Hart saw his individual contributions jump from $342,000 in February to $3 million in March following his New Hampshire victory. In 1988, Gephardt borrowed in an attempt to capitalize on his early success in Iowa but did not experience a sharp increase in individual contributions, probably because of the heavy front-loading of the 1988 primaries; Super Tuesday occurred before most contributors had much time to react to the outcomes of Iowa and New Hampshire" (1991, 101). If contributors did not have enough time to react to the results in early primaries, neither did later voters. Moreover, front-loading meant that the candidates did not have time to visit all of the states involved in Super Tuesday in the short interval, and so they relied more on television advertisements than before.

The year 1992 did show a decline in front-loading in presidential primaries as shown in the figures. Yet, these graphs are misleading since they omit caucus states. Despite the decrease in front-loading of primaries in 1992, 31 states held primaries or caucuses by the end of March of that year (more than half). Moreover, front-loading of presidential primaries was reinvigorated in 1996, and in the 2000 primaries delegate compression for the Republicans surpassed the compression achieved in 1988. Notably, delegate compression in both 1996 and 2000 equaled or superceded 1988 levels because of front-loading. In the 2000 primary season fifteen states held primaries or caucuses on Super Tuesday on March 7. Although this mega primary included less states than the 1988 Super Tuesday, it effectively ended the primary season since larger states such as California, New York, Ohio, and Massachusetts, with more delegates at stake, moved their primaries from later dates to March 7. In fact, Kansas, which had scheduled a Republican caucus after Super Tuesday on April 4, canceled their primary due to a lack of relevance, unbeknown to the leading Republican presidential nominee. The Associated Press reported:

> George W. Bush claimed victory in Tuesday's Kansas primary with thanks to all the voters who came out to support him. One problem: the primary had been canceled in February. "Thank you Pennsylvania, Wisconsin and Kansas," the Texas governor said in a statement issued by his campaign. The release said Tuesday's victories were "adding to a groundswell of grass-roots support for his campaign to the White House." Republican Bush and Democrat Al Gore did coast to victories in Pennsylvania and Wisconsin. But Kansas officials, citing a tight budget and probably lack of relevance so late in the primary season, had done away with their primary. (April 6, 2000)

TABLE 2.2.   2000 Presidential Primary and Caucus Schedule

Date	States with Primaries	States with Caucuses
January 24		Iowa
February 1	New Hampshire	
February 5		Delaware (Democrat)
February 8		Delaware (Republican)
February 19	South Carolina (Republican)	
February 22	Arizona (Republican), Michigan (Republican)	
February 29	Virginia (Republican), Washington	North Dakota (Republicans)
March 7	California, Connecticut, Georgia, Maine, Maryland, Massachusetts, Missouri, New York, Ohio, Rhode Island, Vermont	Hawaii (Democrat), Idaho (Democrat), Minnesota (Republican), North Dakota (Democrat)
March 9		South Carolina (Democrat)
March 10	Colorado, Utah	Wyoming (Republican) Democrats Abroad
March 11	Arizona (Democrat)	Michigan (Democrat)
March 14	Florida, Louisiana (Democrat), Mississippi, Oklahoma, Tennessee, Texas	Louisiana (Republican)
March 21	Illinois	
March 25		Wyoming (Democrat)
April 4	Pennsylvania, Wisconsin	
April 22		Kansas (Democrat)
May 2	Indiana, North Carolina, Washington D.C.	
May 9	Nebraska, West Virginia	
May 16	Oregon	
May 19		Alaska (Republican), Hawaii (Republican), Nevada (Democrat)
May 20		Alaska (Democrat)
May 23	Arkansas, Idaho, Kentucky	
May 25		Nevada (Republican), Kansas (Republican)
June 3		Virginia (Democrat)
June 6	Alabama, Montana, New Jersey, New Mexico, South Dakota	

Note: States are listed in both columns when the different parties use different procedures.

Despite the Republican efforts, 2000 was even more compressed due the number of larger states that their primary or caucus on Super Tuesday. Table 2.2 presents the primary schedule for 2000.

In summary, by 2000 the plebiscitary system had evolved into a virtual national primary through front-loading.[17] While in 1976, 1980, and 1984 primaries were drawn-out enough for some information to be conveyed about lesser-known candidates to later voters, the 2000 primaries were designed for the success of well-known front-runners.

Views of the State of Primaries

Should There Be a Return to Convention Rule?

Our analysis so far of the evolution of the presidential nomination process has demonstrated both the rise of the plebiscitary system, the idiosyncratic sequence of primaries that developed and the nonrepresentativeness of early voters, and the tendency for a virtual national primary to result from excessive front-loading of state primaries.

The dominance of direct primaries has had numerous critics and supporters, particularly in the 1980s. On the one hand, Polsby (1983) argues that the reforms have led to less desirable nominees and more problematic consequences for the role of parties in American politics. He notes that the openness of the caucus process and primaries gives a stronger role to activists who may be ideologically extreme ("purists") and has significantly reduced the roles played by party leaders. Keeter and Zukin (1983) contend that voters are making choices that are uninformed and thus worse than those which would have been made by party elites. Epstein (1983), in contrast, observes that the evidence on the types of candidates is based on too few data points, that the old process led to a number of disastrous nominees, and that the other consequences are more complex. And we have already reviewed the evidence that voters learn through the primary process (Alvarez and Glasgow 1997; Bartels 1988; Popkin 1991). Finally, Abramowitz and Stone (1983), based on surveys of party activists selected from caucuses in 1980, demonstrate that they are not purists but are also concerned with the electability of candidates as well.

Regardless of whether the critics of the new Plebiscitary System are correct, most recognize with Epstein (1983) that it is highly unlikely that the presidential nomination process will move away from rank-and-file participation to again be controlled by party leaders in restricted caucuses and conventions. Even the addition of superdelegates has not led to much change since many of these make commitments to particular candidates prior to the conventions. The central question facing reformers currently is whether to formally legislate procedures for candidate nominations at the federal level. As we have seen, the trend has been toward a virtual national primary with states front-loading primaries and caucuses extremely close to the first-in-the-nation Iowa and New Hampshire contests and in some cases attempting to challenge their opening status. Front-loading seems to advantage well-known front-runner candidates. On the other hand, when primaries are drawn-out there is empirical evidence that voters learn information about candidates that allows them to make what may be more informed decisions. Yet drawn-out primaries give early voters an opportunity to perhaps influence the results of the sequential voting, early voters who are not representative of the general national party membership.

How Can Primaries Be Reformed?

A number of reformers take as given the plebiscitary system of presidential nominations and address the question of how to devise a more "sensible" alternative. Essentially, the free-for-all in scheduling that has resulted in front-loading and earlier and earlier campaigning is viewed as costly to both candidates and states alike. Reform—regulation of the primary system into an easily understood and "fair" schedule—has been proposed by a number of policymakers. The principal two alternative types are a set of regional primaries or one single national primary.

Plans for regional primaries would schedule them approximately two to three weeks apart with an order randomly determined to some extent at first. While regional primaries have endogenously arisen as in the Southern Super Tuesday primaries, the Eastern states' "Junior Tuesday," and the movement toward "Western" primaries as a bloc early in the season, these have also been part of the front-loading process as groups of states jockey together for a bigger role in the nomination process. A standardized regional primary system, in contrast, is expected to increase the length between primaries. Regional primaries are believed to be advantageous in that candidates would be able to campaign in one area of the country at a time and voters may gain information through the primary process. Regional primaries are an enforced sequential voting process. On February 12, 1999, the National Secretaries of State approved a proposal for regional primaries in 2004. It would be a rotating system of four regions as divided in table 2.3 with Iowa and New Hampshire's contests held prior to the regional contests. It remains to be seen whether the plan will be passed, as the Associated Press of February 13, 1999, reported: "they face a formidable task in getting approval of 48 states and both major political parties."

At first glance, a national primary would seem to be a legislated version of the result of front-loading. However, it is possible that a national primary held shortly before the conventions would not advantage well-known and well-financed candidates as front-loading does. That is, a national primary later in the season would give voters national exposure to more candidates than the current front-loaded system because of the time allowed for candidates to campaign.[18] However, it may not be possible for voters to learn at a national level about more than one or two well-known candidates.

Our focus in this book is not on the debate over whether the influence of

TABLE 2.3.   National Secretaries of State Proposed Primary Schedule for 2004

Regions	States in Regions[a]
East	Connecticut, Delaware, Maine, Maryland, Massachusetts, New Jersey, New York, Pennsylvania, Rhode Island, Vermont, West Virginia, and the District of Columbia
South	Alabama, Arkansas, Florida, Georgia, Kentucky, Louisiana, Mississippi, North Carolina, Oklahoma, South Carolina, Tennessee, Texas, Virginia, Puerto Rico, and the Virgin Islands
Midwest	Illinois, Indiana, Kansas, Michigan, Minnesota, Missouri, Nebraska, North Dakota, Ohio, South Dakota, and Wisconsin
West	Alaska, Arizona, California, Colorado, Hawaii, Idaho, Montana, Nevada, New Mexico, Oregon, Utah, Washington, Wyoming and Guam

Source: Associated Press, February 13, 1999.

[a]New Hampshire and Iowa would hold their primaries before the regional schedule—the primary in each state of a given region would be held on or soon after the first Tuesday of March, April, May and June of presidential election years. Not all states would necessarily hold their contest on the same day. After the voting, the region that goes first would go last the next election cycle, and the second region would move up.

primaries and the Democratic reforms of 1968 are good or bad for parties and for the outcomes, but on the comparison of a system with front-loading, a virtual national primary, versus a system in which primaries are sequentially separated. We take as given that primaries are the method by which presidential nominees are selected. Thus, our analysis is also a comparison of the two reform proposals: regional sequentially organized primaries versus a single national primary.

Our work does not just apply to the different presidential primary systems. That is, our analysis applies more generally to other elections where voting is sequential, as in mail-in and early balloting. Interestingly, there are important parallels between the sequential voting in presidential primaries and mail-in and early balloting. In the next chapter, we discuss the evolution of mail-in and early voting in U.S. elections and the perceived pluses and minuses of these developments.

CHAPTER 3

Ballot Boxes at the Mall and the Post Office

Election night in New York City, November 3, 1998, was not a happy one for the candidates for attorney general in New York state. Both Republican incumbent Dennis C. Vacco and Democratic challenger Eliot L. Spitzer had little to say. The outcome of the election would depend on a count of more than 200,000 absentee ballots, still trickling in from all over the world. How would these votes turn out? Some had been mailed, and *returned,* as early as the beginning of October. In the meantime, important campaign events had taken place. Shockingly, Dr. Barnett Slepian, a gynecologist in Buffalo who performed abortions, was shot in the back while standing in his kitchen on Friday, October 23. In a debate the Sunday after the murder, pro-abortion candidate Spitzer attacked anti-abortion advocate Vacco for disassembling the Office of Reproductive Rights, which investigates threats and crimes against abortion clinics and for failing to enforce a court order to protect the clinic where Slepian worked. On election night it appeared to both candidates that the voters that mattered were voters who had chosen before Slepian's murder and asked themselves the same question: "Will the large proportion of upstate absentee voters help Vacco?"[1]

Concerns about the effects of sequential voting led Congress to legislate a uniform federal election day for the selection of electoral college delegates in 1845 and later for members of Congress in 1872. Most states, like New York, also hold other state elections on the same day. Yet, not everyone voted on the same day in November 1998. Some voted almost a month before the election. How has this happened and why? In this chapter, we consider the history and current use of mail-in and early balloting.

A Country at War and on the Move

During the Civil War, many states adopted temporary laws allowing soldiers to vote absentee because of anxiety about the inability of absent voters to participate. Miller 1948 reported that 5.7 percent of the national vote in 1864 was cast by absentee ballot. These measures were generally rescinded after the war. But with the expansion of the railroad, significant numbers of civilians became disfranchised by elections held on a single day, and states began to allow civilian absentee voting as the century closed—Vermont was first in 1896. Kansas followed suit in 1901 with an absentee balloting law, which applied only to railroad employees. In 1913, absentee voting laws were passed in four more states (Minnesota, Missouri, Nebraska, and North Dakota), and by 1924 all but four states allowed some absentee voting.[2]

In 1917 Kettleborough reported on the reasons for the rapid increase in absentee voting statutes in the early twentieth century:

> During the last four years there has been a marked tendency throughout the country to extend the right of voting to electors who are necessarily absent from their voting places on election day. With one notable exception, this tendency seems to be inseparably connected with the changing economic conditions of the country. Thousands of men are now constantly employed in the operation of railroad trains; the nature of their business necessarily requires their absence from home on election as well as other days, with no opportunity, in many cases of casting their votes either at the beginning or at the end of their runs. Traveling salesman [*sic*], railway mail clerks and other persons who are regularly or occasionally absent on business have been subjected to the same inconvenience. To these economic causes has been added during the past year, the mobilization of the militia on the southern border, just prior to the presidential election. (320)

These absentee balloting measures differed across states in their application to civilians and in the ability of voters to vote outside the state. Virginia's law serves as an example of a liberal statute; it allowed absent voters to "vote in any place either in the United States or in any foreign country at any primary or general election" (320). Nevertheless, absentee balloting was to be used only when a voter was expected to be absent—not just because voting early might be more convenient or preferred.

Expanding the Franchise

Liberalized absentee ballot laws increased in the 1970s. In a general sense, the expansion of absentee balloting privileges is part of the general enlargement of the voting franchise that took place after the passage of the Voting Rights Act of 1965. That is, like the decrease in the voting age, easier access to absentee balloting was designed to increase the ability of all voters to participate in electoral contests. The 1970 Voting Rights Act explicitly required that U.S. citizens be allowed to vote for president and vice president even though they had failed to satisfy a state's registration requirement (at that time, for example, Tennessee had a year residency requirement for voter registration), and it established uniform standards for absentee registration and balloting in presidential elections.[3] And in *Dunn and Blumstein* (1972), the U.S. Supreme Court struck down lengthy residency requirements—like Tennessee's—for federal elections.[4] Caldeira and Patterson record: "Beginning in the mid-1970s, states increasingly began to adopt provisions for absentee mail registration. And during the 1970s, most states added, broadened, and liberalized laws on absentee voting (see Smolka, 1982)" (1985, 769).

Absentee ballots have been decisive in a number of elections as in the New York contest between Spitzer and Vacco. In that contest, absentee ballots revealed a win for Spitzer, although Vacco did not concede defeat until the middle of December.[5] Caldeira and Patterson discuss how in 1982 Republican George "Duke" Deukmejian defeated Democrat Tom Bradley in the gubernatorial election: "On election day, 2 November 1982, Bradley won more than half of the two-party vote. His vote exceeded that of Deukmejian by a razor-thin margin of nearly 20,000. Yet, to the chagrin of Democrats in the Golden State, Deukmejian 'snatched victory from the jaws of defeat.' When officials had counted absentee ballots, Deukmejian won the final reckoning by garnering over 113,000 more of the votes cast in absentia than had been mailed in for Bradley" (1985, 766). But this is not the first time in American elections that absentee ballots have made such a difference. Caldeira and Patterson report:

> It is said, for instance, that Franklin D. Roosevelt lost the 1944 election in New Jersey on election day, but that his support was so great in the absentee vote of soldiers that the electoral vote of that state went to Roosevelt instead of the Republican candidate, Thomas E. Dewey (Miller 1948, 106). In 1960, John F. Kennedy carried California by a narrow margin on election day, but when absentee votes were counted Richard M. Nixon won the state's electoral vote by a 36,000-vote margin (Owens, Costantini, and Weschler 1970, 97). . . . More commonly, absentee votes can contribute to the victor's electoral margin. In 1966, when Ronald Reagan was first elected governor of California, dislodging incumbent Edmund "Pat" Brown, Republican candidate Reagan won 58 percent of the two-party vote, but his support was 65 percent among absentees (Owens, Costantini, and Weschler 1970, 98). In Iowa in 1982, Republican Terry E. Branstad won 53% of the vote on election day against Democrat Roxanne Conlin, but he garnered almost 55 percent of the absentee votes. (1985, 769)

Absence Becomes a Matter of Timing

Liberalization of the definition of absentee balloting has, in some states, evolved into an extended voting period, resulting in "early voting" with many voters choosing while a campaign is still raging. How has this happened? It has occurred largely to increase turnout and participation in electoral contests. It first began to appear in a few local elections where officials despaired of declining turnout and interest in special ballot measures like Denver's Regional Transit Authority discussed in chapter 1. Magleby 1987 reports that the first such completely mail-in balloting took place in Monterey County, California, for a small special district election in April 1977. Other localities have subsequently experimented with mail-in balloting elections: according to Hamilton 1988, thousands of substate, often nonpartisan, vote-by-mail elections have been held.

The Lone Star State Experiments

In a number of states, liberalization of early and mail-in balloting to voters at large at the state level has occurred as well. Texas presents an interesting case study of the process of change from simultaneous to sequential voting elections. Rosenfield relates this history:

> Early voting . . . began in the State of Texas. It did not spring full grown to life, but began unobtrusively in 1963 with a provision that allowed one temporary branch absentee voting location in counties where the county seat was not the largest town in the county. In 1967 the County Commissioners Court was permitted to establish additional temporary branch absentee voting locations in the county at their discretion, but evidently few if any counties took advantage of this obscure permissive provision.
>
> In 1986 a Texas legislator was irritated by the fact that he had to stretch the truth in stating that he expected to be absent on election day in order to vote by absentee ballot. In 1987 he introduced legislation abolishing the requirement for stating a reason for personal appearance absentee voting. . . . County Clerks were mandated to provide in-person absentee voting at the Clerk's office . . . and at any permanent substations of the Clerk's office from the 20th day through the 4th day before an election. . . .
>
> In 1988 another legislator was angered when he almost missed being able to vote absentee because he arrived to vote on the last day just five minutes before the County Clerk's office closed at 4:30. In 1989 he introduced legislation to require the most populous Texas counties to remain open for extended hours during the last week of absentee voting. . . .
>
> In 1991 the Texas legislature . . . made the changes creating the early voting system that has attracted nationwide attention. They changed terminology, substituting "early voting" for "absentee voting" to accommodate the law that allows any voter to vote early by personal appearance. They authorized political subdivisions in any county to establish tempo-

rary branch early voting locations for shorter hours. This freed counties to create temporary branches at many different locations, including nongovernmental locations, each operating for a few days or even for a few hours. . . . These changes facilitated use of store hours for voting at times more convenient to voters and led to increased use of locations such as shopping malls and grocery stores, dubbed "retail voting." (1994, 7–8)

Texas's early voting system has been widely emulated; at least 21 states had adopted similar procedures by the end of 1998, although these are typically not mandated for counties but rather are options available to local election officials.

Absence as a Matter of State Citizenship

Data on existing absentee and early voting statutes as of April 1999 are presented in table 3.1. There is significant variation across states in these statutes. Almost half the states (23) allow no early balloting, restricting absentee voting to those who meet particular requirements. Eleven states have restrictions on absentee ballots but allow some early voting, while nine states have no restrictions on eligibility for absentee ballots but do not allow early voting. Eight states have the most liberal early and mail-in balloting statutes. Notably all these states are west of the Mississippi River. The length of time allowed for absentee balloting also varies by state: in North Carolina and Kentucky absentee ballots are mailed out 50 days prior to an election, while in Louisiana, Nevada, and Washington they are mailed out 20 days prior. Early voting takes place from 45 days prior to an election in Oregon to 3 days prior to an election in Maryland, Virginia, and Oklahoma.

While Texas's early balloting system extensively uses satellite polling places open days before an official election date, Oregon has also expanded into early voting by instituting mail-in balloting at a statewide level, the first state to use mail-in voting for statewide elections. Oregon first began to allow voting-by-mail in elections that did not involve candidates or were scheduled on the same date as a primary or general election with candidates in 1981. Voting-by-mail expanded over the following decade, and by 1995 presidential preference primary elections were required to be conducted by mail. In 1996 the state used mail-in ballots for the first statewide general election involving candidates: the special election to replace U.S. senator Robert Packwood. On November 3, 1998, Oregon voters approved by 69 percent a vote-by-mail system for all statewide elections. Under the new system, Oregon voters will receive ballots in the mail not more than 20 days before an election. The completed ballots can be deposited at any officially designated place, or voters can vote in person at their county election office on election day if they choose.

TABLE 3.1. State Regulations on Absentee, Early, and Mail-in Voting, December 1998

	Number of Days Prior to Election Absentee Ballots are Mailed	Number of Days Prior to Election Early Voting is Allowed
Standard Eligibility Restrictions on Absentee Voting without Early Voting		
Alabama	40	—[a]
Arkansas	25	—
Connecticut	30	—
Delaware	45	—
Florida	35	—
Illinois	45	—
Minnesota	30	—
Missouri	42	—
Nebraska	35	—
New Hampshire	30	—
New Jersey	40	—
New York	32	—
North Carolina	50	—
Rhode Island	21	—
Vermont	35	—
Wisconsin	30	—
Expanded Eligibility Restrictions on Absentee Voting without Early Voting		
Georgia	45	—
Kentucky	50	—
Michigan	45	—
Mississippi	45	—
Ohio	35	—
Pennsylvania	45	—
South Carolina	45	—
Standard Eligibility Restrictions on Absentee Voting with Early Voting		
Massachusetts	35	14
North Dakota	40	30
South Dakota	42	42
Utah	35	35
Expanded Eligibility Restrictions on Absentee Voting with Early Voting		
Washington, D.C.	35	14
Indiana	45	7
Louisiana	20	7
Maryland	35	3
Tennessee	45	12 to 5[b]
Virginia	45	3
West Virginia	42	15 to 3[b]

TABLE 3.1.—*Continued*

	Number of Days Prior to Election Absentee Ballots are Mailed	Number of Days Prior to Election Early Voting is Allowed
Any Registered Voting Absentee Voting without Early Voting		
Arizona	33	—
California	29	—
Hawaii	35	—
Idaho	35	—
Maine	45	—
Montana	45	—
Nevada	20	—
Washington	20	—
Wyoming	40	—
Any Registered Voting Absentee Voting with Early Voting		
Alaska	26	15
Colorado	30	10
Iowa	40	3
Kansas	45	20 to 7[b]
New Mexico	40	20
Oklahoma	30	3
Oregon	45	45
Texas	45	17 to 4[b]

Note:
Standard Eligibility Requirements for Absentee Voting:
  1. Temporary absence from the area on election day (the area consists of county, state, or precinct for reasons including school, vacation, temporarily living in another county, township or state).
  2. Some physical ailment prevents a voter from the polls on election day (if a voter is sick, ill, disabled, in nursing home, in hospital, or is emotional or mental impaired).
  3. Other obligations preventing a voter from the polls on election day (such as work, jury duty, law official business, election official, in jail, religious reasons).
Expanded Eligibility Requirements for Absentee Voting adds age to the Standard Eligibility Requirements
[a]The dash (—) indicates this restriction is not applicable.
[b]When the number of days for early voting is an interval, the last number indicates the number of days before the election that early voting is halted.

The liberalization of mail-in and other early balloting procedures has changed the nature of election contests in those states and localities where they have been used. As Rosenfield comments: "One known effect of early voting is that it changes the dynamics and strategy of political campaigns. What is not clear is exactly how it changes campaigning. Some Texas counties comment that the major challenge presented by early voting to candidates and voters alike has been the transition from focusing on a *single* election day high-point to focusing on a series of high-points created by *multiple* early voting election days in addition to a climax on election day" (1994, 5; emphasis in the original).

Early voting procedures have made the choices in these elections sequential rather than simultaneous.

Making Turnout Fun

The principal advantage and reason for allowing mail-in and early balloting is an anticipated increase in political participation and turnout. Rosenfield summarizes:

> Proponents say that early voting will increase turnout and make voting more accessible and convenient to under-represented groups, such as elderly, disabled, and young people, and to people who find it difficult to get to a central election office because of distance, lack of transportation, or nontraditional work schedules; that it is advantageous in areas that frequently experience bad weather conditions on election day. (1994, 3)

Does sequential (early and mail-in) balloting lead to an increase in participation? Before addressing this question, we consider the determinants of voter participation in elections and how early and mail-in balloting can affect voter participation.

The Paradox of Participation

Probably one of the most studied of political behaviors in American politics is the decision to vote. Voting, as Fiorina 1995 and Aldrich 1993 discuss, is a low-cost/low-benefit decision, which makes the choice, some would argue, subject to a number of factors that seem unrelated to the standard benefit/cost calculation. That is, the standard calculus of voting (see Riker and Ordeshook 1968) argues that individuals will vote if the expected benefits from voting exceed the costs. Formally, a voter will vote if the following is true:

$$\Delta P \times B > C$$

where ΔP is the effect of the voter's choice on the outcome of the election (a function of the probability that one vote is decisive), B is the benefit the voter receives from electing a more favored candidate than who would win if the voter chooses not to vote, and C is the cost of voting. The cost of voting is the opportunity cost of going to the polls. In any large election, ΔP is likely to be very small, and thus most argue that if voters are participating for investment reasons (to affect the benefits he or she will receive), then no one should vote (the paradox of participation or of not voting).

Since Downs 1957 first noted the paradox of not voting, researchers have considered many possible explanations of why voters choose to turn out. This literature is reviewed in Morton 1991, Aldrich 1993, and Jackman 1993. Typically, the paradox is resolved in an ad hoc fashion by adding a positive D term to $\Delta P \times B$ that represents citizen duty or the psychological benefit that individuals receive from the act of voting that is independent of the outcome of the election (see Riker and Ordeshook 1968). This is sometimes also thought of as the "consumption benefits of voting." Nevertheless, explaining turnout as determined by adding in an unexplained "citizen duty" begs the question of why turnout varies over time and with election type, closeness of election, and the stakes voters have in elections.

One important aspect of this calculus of voting is that it ignores the strategic nature of the act—that is, if all voters choose not to vote, then the probability of being decisive for each is equal to 1! Palfrey and Rosenthal 1983, 1985, and Ledyard 1984 have explored models of elections where voters make turnout decisions strategically, recognizing the cross effects of their decisions. Ledyard shows that when two candidates offer distinct positions then rational, investment-motivated turnout is positive. However, as the electorate grows large—approaches infinity—turnout levels approach zero (Palfrey and Rosenthal 1985).

Turnout as a Group Pastime

There is empirical evidence that voters are motivated in making participation decisions by the investment benefits (the differences between candidates that affect them) and the costs of voting in making participation decisions. For example, Filer, Kenny, and Morton 1993 find that voters' turnout is related to the effect the election may have on their after-tax income—voters at high and low ends of the income distribution and who are more likely to be affected by governmental redistribution are more likely to vote, all other things equal. Filer et al. also find that voters are more likely to turn out when elections are close (the probability of being decisive is higher) and are less likely to vote when measures of the cost of voting increase. How can we reconcile this empirical evidence with the paradox of participation?

One solution is to view participation as a group-level decision: for a group of like-minded voters participation of the group can affect the election outcome and should be motivated by the closeness of the election, the differences between the candidates, and the costs of voting. Morton 1987, 1991 and Uhlaner 1989 make this argument. The group explanation of turnout suggests that the unexplained "citizen duty" component of individual turnout benefits consists of individualized incentives provided by the group to voters for participating (see Olson 1965), incentives that may be social in character. Under this explanation, then, electoral participation is a function of the closeness of an election, the benefits and costs to voters, and the ability of groups to mobilize their members. Mobilization in elections is an important aspect of the voting process.

Empirical research on voter turnout has shown the importance of mobilization. Caldeira, Patterson, and Markko 1985, in an examination of turnout in congressional elections in 1978, find that political mobilization is a significant determinant of voter turnout. Rosenstone and Hansen 1993 present a detailed empirical study of the relationship between mobilization and participation.

Does Early Balloting Work?

As noted above, most of the advantage of early voting is that it lowers the cost of participation—by allowing balloting at malls or by mail, there is no question that the act of voting is easier and less costly than when elections are held on one day at specified locations. Thus, for many reasons, early and mail-in balloting should make it easier for voters to be mobilized and should result in an increase in turnout, particularly among voters who previously were unable to vote on election day. There is some empirical support for this argument. Magleby 1987 studied mail-in balloting in seven cities and found that turnout increased significantly in six. He concluded: "Jurisdictions which have used a mail ballot election have had a turnout rate of 19 percent over that which we would expect for a polling place election, holding all other variables constant" (88). Patterson and Caldeira 1985 studied the effect of liberal absentee voting laws on participation in larger elections in California and Iowa. They find that while absentee measures have a positive effect on turnout, the effect is strongly influenced by the degree of partisan mobilization of the electorate.

Other researchers have conducted analyses of turnout in Texas (Stein and Garcia-Monet 1997; Stein 1998) and Oregon (Traugott 1997; Berinsky, Burns, and Traugott 1998), the two states with the most extensive early (Texas) and mail-in (Oregon) balloting experiences. Stein and Garcia-Monet study early voting in the 1992 presidential election in Texas and found a positive effect on turnout although they were not able to determine the extent that the effect was due to mobilization rather than the advent of early voting. Traugott 1997 found that voting-by-mail "has not systematically increased turnout in Oregon, although this seems well-explained by existing models of voting behavior in the United States. The convenience of voting-by-mail does stimulate turnout in lower turnout elections like primaries and referenda, and it does seem to have its greatest impact among groups of voters who ordinarily are least likely to vote. But turnout in general elections in Oregon is already so high, there is less room for significant impact there."

Who Votes Early?

Are Early Voters Different from Election Day Voters?

If the turnout effect of early and mail-in balloting is a factor of mobilization efforts of groups and in particular political parties, then what types of voters are more likely to be reached? As Rosenfield 1994 notes, some advocates argue that these measures will reach voters who are less likely to vote otherwise and increase turnout of underrepresented voters in elections that previously did not have early and mail-in balloting. Yet, in fact the empirical evidence does not support this conclusion. Oliver 1996 made a cross-state comparison of 1992 turnout levels as a function of absentee voting eligibility, mobilization efforts and types of voters. He concludes: "Liberalizing absentee eligibility has produced its intended effect on increasing turnout, but not by encouraging turnout among those groups less likely to vote like the young or uneducated. Higher turnout is the consequence of political parties targeting and reaching those individuals more likely to vote anyway, i.e., registered voters" (510). He also finds that the voters most likely to be so mobilized are elderly and Republican.

Stein 1998 compares election day with early voters in Texas's 1994 gubernatorial election. He finds:

> The sharpest distinctions between election-day and early voters were observed for attitudinal (i.e., interest in politics, partisanship, and ideology) rather than for demographic traits. . . . these findings underscore the view that early voting is largely a function of convenience and partisan interest (i.e., those who arrive at a vote choice early in the political campaign). (67)

Figure 3.1 shows the relationship between reported strength of partisanship of voters in Texas's 1994 gubernatorial election and measures of early voting.[6] Early voters are more strongly partisan than election day voters, and mail-in voters are even more strongly partisan.

Stein's results support the implication that early voting is largely used in Texas to mobilize already registered and committed voters. Stein concludes:

> Candidates and their parties might prefer to turn out their core supporters early in order to concentrate late campaign efforts on voters with weak partisan ties who require stronger issue and candidate appeals in order to win their votes. . . . If candidates use this strategy, I would not expect early voting to mobilize a significant number of new voters, nor would I expect to observe any net partisan bias to early voting. The effect of this strategy would be to allow parties and their candidates to more effectively compete for the swing and nonpartisan voter. (1998, 68)

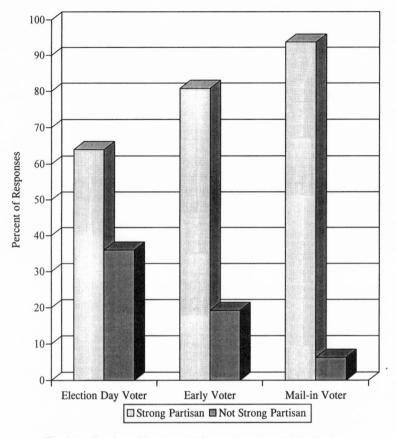

Fig. 3.1.   Partisanship strength by early and mail-in balloting

Berinsky, Burns, and Traugott 1998 analyzed data from a panel study of voter behavior over five mail-in elections in Oregon. They collected detailed data on the subjects' voting histories and used a multistate duration empirical model to analyze their predictions. They found results that supported the conclusions of Stein 1998 and Oliver 1996 about the identity of early voters as those who are typically strong partisans and normally likely to vote. Berinsky, Burns, and Traugott deduce:

VBM [voting-by-mail] mobilized those already predisposed to vote—those individuals who are long-term residents and who are registered partisans—to turn out at higher rates than before. This process likely occurs because voting across a twenty-day period reduces the impact of idiosyncratic factors that inhibit a likely voter from going to a polling place on a particular day. The policy change had little positive impact on those without resources—on the mobile or those with low levels of education or campaign interest. To the extent that VBM changed the Oregon electorate, it simply enabled those who were resource rich to remain, more consistently, in the electorate. Of course, this non-partisan change could have tremendous partisan consequences in some jurisdictions, to the extent that the newly mobilized and surprisingly retained resource rich voters are of a particular partisan stripe. In Oregon, however, there is no evidence of such an indirect partisan bias. (1998, 26)

Voting and Knowledge

Even if early outcomes are not revealed to later voters, with early and mail-in balloting, voters will choose with different types of information about the election. In Denver, a third of the voters chose before the unusual fall snowstorm that provided new evidence on the benefits of light rail. Events occur during elections that can alter voters' knowledge of candidate positions and their preferences as a consequence. How much does information variation across voters in sequential voting lead to different outcomes than when elections are simultaneous? While it may be possible to control news reports with projections based on early voting results, it is not possible for the world to remain frozen during a sequential voting election. Unlikely events like terrorist strikes or scandals of corruption can occur in the midst of an election contest.

Further, if early and later voters have different preferences they may also have different types of information about candidates. Candidates will campaign differently since they know that the different voters are interested in different things. Candidates who are extremist may be more likely to make themselves well-known to early voters, whereas moderates may appeal to undecideds who are more likely to be later voters.

Who Votes Late?

The empirical evidence then suggests that to date early and mail-in balloting does have a positive impact on turnout, but that this impact appears primarily to affect voters who are most likely to vote normally but whose votes are less reliable when elections are held on a single day. There seems to be no evidence from the elections in Oregon and Texas or in Oliver's (1996) cross-state study that these measures increase participation of other voters, independents and/or those generally unrepresented in elections without early and mail-in balloting. Could these measures have a negative effect on their participation?

As discussed above, part of the calculus of voting is the anticipated effect of votes on the electoral outcome. When voting takes place over a period of time, even a day, the expected effect of a single vote can vary when later voters have information about the outcome of earlier balloting. A continual concern in presidential elections has been the effect of media reports based on Eastern and Midwestern voting on the participation rate of Western voters. Jackson 1983 and Delli Carpini 1984 analyze the effect of election night reporting on the 1980 contest. Both find that in 1980, reports that the election outcome was largely decided did decrease turnout in Western states. Jackson notes, however, that the effect is primarily because the results from early voting were unexpected, and so they changed the expected value of a vote as calculated prior to the election. Jackson contends:

> In the case of a lopsided contest, in which the projections are easily made before poll closings, such as the contests of 1972, 1964, and probably 1956 (if the technology had been available), people whose decision to vote is influenced by the certainty of the election's expected outcome will already have taken most of this factor into account and the impact of a confirming election day projection will be modest. . . .
>
> The early reporting of projections may only alter turnout in elections in which the projections differ from prior expectations. Elections in which people anticipate a close race, but in which the early returns and projections indicate the opposite, are the situations we expect to see a drop in turnout directly related to the media's coverage. The 1980, and possibly the 1960, elections fit this category. . . . For the converse case, in which people expect a one-sided election that in fact turns out to be close, such as the elections of 1948 and 1968, early reporting of this closeness may spur people to vote who might not have under the expectation of no contest. (1983, 631)

Jackson concludes: "What analysis can point out, as we do here, is that people's likelihood of voting is related to their perception of the value of their vote in determining the election's outcome. Events that alter that perceived value alter turnout" (633).

Early and mail-in balloting of some committed voters, if reported to undecideds, may either increase or decrease turnout depending on the effect such reporting has on the perception of election closeness. Moreover, if reporting on early voting results becomes the norm this is likely to have perverse effects on voters' incentives in timing their votes. That is, voters who want to be sure that their vote counts may find themselves voting earlier and earlier, just as states are front-loading presidential primaries. Conversely, voters who are not inclined to be interested in elections may wait until they have information from early balloting before deciding whether the contest is a worthwhile investment of their time. Jackson makes a similar point with respect to the effect that reporting on East Coast voting can have on West Coast voters' incentives: "Given the publicity on the topic, people may have learned to wait until late on election day to vote knowing they can find out before the polls close if the election is unexpectedly close" (1983, 633).

How relevant is the issue of reporting during an election for early and mail-in balloting? The early voting statutes generally clearly control the counting and revelation of the results. In most cases the early ballots are not opened until after the election is concluded or at the same time as the other ballots. Nevertheless, this does not prevent the news media from polling individuals, asking them whether they have voted yet and how they have voted. While no famous examples exist of this type of reporting yet, early and mail-in balloting is relatively new, and the incentives for projections may overcome a norm against this type of reporting. As quoted in chapter 1, news media decision makers, like Mike Devlin of Oregon, recognize their ability to gain this information and its value.

It should be noted that such reporting may have a positive benefit if voters do learn by voting. That is, there may be some learning when voters vote sequentially; later voters can find out the outcome of earlier choices and may be able to infer information about candidates from earlier voting and learn by voting, much as advocates of drawn-out presidential primaries believe that later voters can learn by the results of early contests.

Presidential Primaries, Early Voting, and Timing

While our discussion in the previous chapter emphasized how front-loading of presidential primaries is resulting in contests that are more like simultaneous voting, our argument in this chapter has been that early and mail-in balloting are making other elections more like sequential voting. Yet the time during which voting takes place in the two systems does not seem that different—that is, the front-loaded primaries of 1996 lasted about as long as the standard early and mail-in balloting period. Is this inconsistent reasoning, then? Moreover, many early and mail-in voters may not be voting *that* early. Many absentee ballots in California are returned to the polling place on election day—sometimes as many as 50 percent, but generally 30 to 40 percent. Approximately 80 to 90 percent are estimated to be returned within seven days of the election. In California, voters are not yet able to vote at early polling stations as in Texas.[7] The Texas survey on early voting shows that of the early voters, 2.9 percent vote four weeks in advance, 7.73 percent three weeks in advance, 34.3 percent two weeks in advance, and 55.07 percent one week in advance. About a third of the surveyed voters voted in advance either at early polling stations or by mail, almost all of them at the early stations. This suggests that when a state has early polling stations at malls, and so on, voters choose earlier than they do when the ballots are mailed in or returned to the polling station on election day.

Our belief is that the difference in scale of elections matters. That is, in a local or even state-level contest in a small state, voting over a few weeks can be equivalent to voting over a few months in a national contest like presidential nominations. The expansion of early and mail-in balloting has made elections in Texas, Oregon, and other jurisdictions where the procedures are expanding in use fundamentally different from the perspective of the candidates and campaign managers. Campaign managers are able to use information from past voting behavior to identify voters who tend to choose early. Political consultant Larry Levine reports about California (a state with only absentee balloting and no early voting at malls):

> While 80% or more of the absentee votes cast their ballots in the last seven days, that still can leave a significant number of people who vote before that time. Missing them in a campaign can be fatal. . . . I can divide the file of likely voters into those with an absentee history and those without. I can even divide the absentee segment based on frequency of voting by mail in specific types of elections. In recent campaigns I have actually created parallel budgets and schedules so people with absentee histories would receive the voter mail, phone calls, etc. one week earlier than those with no absentee history on the theory that most of them would be voting one week earlier than the rest of the universe.[8]

As a result, many of the issues that are relevant in drawn-out presidential primaries are also relevant for these elections. In particular, there is evidence that early voters are not representative of the electorate as a whole, but more partisan. To what extent can these voters determine the outcome of an election? To what extent will information asymmetries across voters make a difference in who is elected? And to what extent can later voters infer information from news reports or projections based on earlier voting? These are questions we address in our experiments described in the remaining chapters. But before we turn to the experimental analysis, we review the literature on formal models of simultaneous and sequential elections and presidential primaries.

CHAPTER 4

Modeling Voting and Sequence

The March 1929 issue of the *Economic Journal* had articles by noted economists J. M. Keynes and Lionel Robbins. It also had an interesting paper by mathematical economist Harold Hotelling on the competition of firms in location as well as price and output. He wondered about the spatial location of companies: assuming that customers are spread out along a single main street or a railroad, where would competing firms locate? His answer—that firms would be drawn to similar and centrist locations—has led to much subsequent research in economic theory. But in addition, the model has had a large influence on our understanding of voting in elections. Hotelling noted that the competition between political parties could be likened to the competition between firms over policy issues, having a similar effect. Much ensuing formal research on voting in elections has resulted as well.[1]

In the tradition of Hotelling and subsequent modelers of voting like Downs 1957, we take a rational choice approach to understanding voter behavior. In our model, voters choose in order to maximize their expected satisfaction. Unlike Hotelling, however, our model does not have strategic political parties or candidates. Instead, we focus on voter choices given a set of candidates and an electoral institution. We also allow for more than two potential candidates and the choices that voters have to make in this context. Most rational choice-based models of elections that have been previously applied to presidential primaries or to voting in large U.S. elections have taken the Hotelling-Downsian approach. Before presenting our model, it is useful to discuss the other formal literature on voting and elections as it relates to the concerns of sequential voting in real-world elections and place the Hotelling-Downsian approach and ours in context.

In the previous two chapters, we explored the worries policymakers have about sequential voting. We focused on two types of sequential voting in elections: sequential voting in drawn-out presidential primaries and sequential voting in elections held over a period of time (early and mail-in balloting). In presidential primaries, the issue is whether front-loaded presidential primaries are better or worse than drawn-out presidential primaries. Front-loaded presidential primaries are hypothesized to lead to the dominance of well-known candidates who may not be the most preferred candidates of all voters. Voters do not have a chance to learn during the presidential primary season. In contrast, drawn-out presidential primaries are believed to advantage early voters' preferences, voters who may not be representative of the entire electorate, which leads to the selection of extremist candidates.

Policymakers have similar worries about the effects of early and mail-in balloting. When voting is sequential, voters make decisions with different degrees and types of information about the candidates depending on when they vote. This may lead to different electoral outcomes. Policymakers also worry about the possibility that early voters, not representative of the electorate and perhaps more partisan or extreme, will dominate election outcomes. In order to address these issues about sequential voting in presidential primaries and in early balloting systems, we need to consider formal models of both a simultaneous voting election and a sequential voting election.

Modeling Simultaneous Voting

First-Generation Models of Elections: Hotelling-Downsian Spatial Competition

Most formal models of elections assume simultaneous voting. The literature examining simultaneous voting is large, and the basics of these models are discussed elsewhere (see in particular Hinich and Munger 1997). It is useful, however, to discuss some of the different types of models of elections in the literature and where our model of voting fits in. First, the earliest models of elections centered on two-candidate or two-party competition (in many of these models candidates and parties are interchangeable labels)—as in the seminal work of Hotelling 1929 and Downs 1957. These are spatial voting models in that candidates or parties choose spatial positions and voters choose the party or candidate whose spatial position is closest to their most preferred policy position. In these models, candidates or parties choose policy positions primarily in order to win elections, although in some they also may care about policy as well (see Calvert 1985; Wittman 1991). Candidates or parties are also generally constrained to enact the policies promised in elections (see Alesina 1987 for an exception).

In the early models, candidates (or parties) and voters have full information about both the chosen policy positions and the preferences of voters. When policy is one-dimensional and voters' preferences over policy are single-peaked (that is, voters have a most preferred policy position or ideal point, and as policy moves further from this ideal point voters' satisfaction or utility from policy declines), then the candidates or parties choose convergent policy positions equal to the ideal point or most preferred policy position of the voter whose

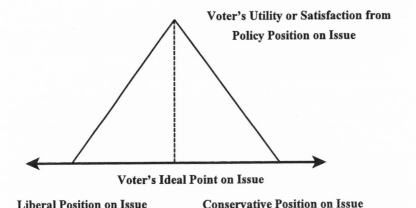

Voter's Utility or Satisfaction from
Policy Position on Issue

Voter's Ideal Point on Issue

Liberal Position on Issue   **Conservative Position on Issue**

Fig. 4.1.   Example of single-peaked preferences

ideal point is at the median of voter ideal points. Figure 4.1 gives an example of a voter with single-peaked preferences.

Of course, while centrist tendencies are obvious features of our two-party competition (some contend that Democratic president Clinton co-opted many Republican positions), there is still strong evidence that the political parties do maintain distinct differences, as demonstrated in Schmidt, Kenny, and Morton 1996. A significant amount of subsequent research has focused on the factors that affect the degree of convergence of parties, factors such as the influence of party elites who may have extreme preferences, policy preferences of candidates, or the potential entry of third parties or candidates. Schmidt, Kenny, and Morton 1996 review this literature.

Unfortunately, when policy is multidimensional, there may not be a stable position or set of positions for candidates or parties to choose—leading some to say that political science is truly the "dismal science" (Riker 1980). In other words, there may be no stable equilibrium or solution to the game between the candidates or parties. The instability occurs because candidates or parties can easily increase their probability of winning by only small moves in policy. That is, when parties or candidates can compete on more than one policy issue, then they can make moves in many directions, and the potential to take away voters is multiplied. Thus, in many cases there are no positions where each candidate or party is choosing optimally given the choice of the other candidate or parties (i.e., a small move is always preferable, and there is simply no solution or prediction as to where parties or candidates will locate!).[2]

Again, there has been a considerable amount of subsequent research to address the evidence of empirical stability of candidate or party competition with the dismal prediction of multidimensional voting models. In models of elections, the principal solution has been to turn to probabilistic voting models where candidates or parties are uncertain about the location of the median voter's ideal point in the electorate due perhaps to a lack of precision in predictions of voter turnout (see Ledyard 1984). When candidates or parties are not certain about the location of the median voter's ideal point, then small moves in policy space are no longer so rewarding. Stable equilibrium policy positions for the candidates or parties can exist. Probabilistic voting models are also attractive for empirical analysis of voting in elections; we have seen a growing use for such study (see Morton 1999 chapter 6 for a review).

Second-Generation Models of Elections: Strategic Voting and Coordination

A second generation of voting models has taken a different approach from the Hotelling-Downsian emphasis on two-party or candidate spatial location competition for votes. In the second generation, the focus has switched from an emphasis on the selection of spatial policy positions to the selection by voters over a set of candidates or parties, generally more than two. Instead of defining voters' utility over policy space and candidates or parties as choosing positions in this space to maximize electoral chances or other motives, in some of these models policy is completely ignored, and voters' preferences are modeled directly over the candidates or parties (see Cox 1997, for example). Others in the second-generation approach assume that the candidates or parties have fixed policy positions or preferences that are known and that voters' utility over these candidates or parties is derived from voters' preferences over policy (as is a possible interpretation of the model of voting we present in the next chapter). In some of these models, called *citizen-candidate* models, each voter can potentially enter as a candidate in an election (see Osborne and Slivinski 1996; Besley and Coate 1997).

While the first-generation election models are characterized by difficulties in finding voting equilibria, the second-generation election models have the opposite problem—multiple equilibria![3] That is, in the second-generation election models there are generally more than two potential candidates or parties. For example, consider a voting model with three candidates, each with a group of voters who strongly prefer one of the candidates as their first choice. It might be like the 1970 U.S. Senate race where Republican incumbent Charles Goodell faced challenges from Democrat Richard Ottinger and Conservative Party candidate James Buckley. Goodell, who had a liberal voting record, and Ottinger each had a group of liberal supporters, while Buckley was supported by conservatives and most Republicans. Although there were more supporters of Goodell and Ottinger than Buckley, suggesting that voters as a majority preferred a liberal senator, Buckley won because these voters could not agree on either Goodell or Ottinger.

There were three possible outcomes in the New York election: liberal voters could have coordinated on Goodell, assuring him victory; liberal voters could have coordinated on Ottinger, assurring him victory; or liberal voters could have divided, splitting their roles between Goodell and Ottinger, resulting in a Buckley win. Thus there were two possible election outcomes where liberal voters coordinated and one where they did not. In the outcome that occurred Goodell and Ottinger supporters voted sincerely for their most preferred candidates.

Similarly, in the second-generation voting models, in many cases there will be equilibria where all the voters will vote sincerely for their first choice—all three candidates will receive votes. But there may also be equilibria where some voters vote strategically for their second preferred candidate (see Myerson and Weber 1993). This is the case in the voting model that we will present in the next chapter.

When voters choose strategically a candidate or party that is not their first preference, we can think of the voters as coordinating with other voters in an electoral coalition—a coalition of voters who choose together to defeat a candidate or party less preferred by all voters in the coalition. Goodell and Ottinger supporters were not able to coordinate in such a coalition. The accent in the second-generation models is on voter coordination and strategy in forming electoral coalitions. This contrasts to the first-generation models, which primarily concentrate on the strategies and choices of office-seeking candidates and parties (generally two), and voters simply choose the candidate or party they prefer (absention is a problem, however, as we have discussed in the previous chapter). One of the stresses of the second-generation models, then, has been on the factors that influence the likelihood of strategic voting and electoral coalition formation in elections. Cox's 1997 study of the effects of different electoral systems on strategic voting and electoral coalition formation is a particularly noteworthy example of this second-generation approach. Table 4.1 summarizes the differences between first- and second-generation formal models of elections.

We also are interested in the effects of electoral systems on electoral coalition formation. That is, we inquire into how sequential versus simultaneous voting affects the likelihood that voters will choose strategically or sincerely and the electoral coalitions that may or may not result. In U.S. elections, our system of plurality rule and other institutions generally provides voters with strong incentives to form coalitions at the electoral stage rather than post-election as in many countries where legislatures are selected using proportional representation systems—that is, where seats in the parliament are given out based on the share of votes that a party receives, and coalition formation often takes place

TABLE 4.1. First- and Second-Generation Formal Models of Elections

	First-Generation Models of Elections (Hotelling-Downsian Spatial Voting Models)	Second-Generation Models of Elections (Cox, Myerson, and Weber, and Citizen-Candidate Models)
Number of parties or candidates modeled	Typically two, sometimes more	Generally more than two
Voter utility functions	Voter preferences are typically defined over policy spaces	Voter preferences are typically defined over candidates or parties directly; sometimes these are derived from policy positions of candidates
Candidate or party motivations and strategic choices	Candidates or parties strategically choose policy positions to maximize expected utility (which may be merely a function or winning but sometimes also policy preferences of candidates or party members)	Candidates or parties have fixed policy positions when policy is modeled—strategic choices of candidates or parties when modeled are typically entry decisions
Voter choices	Typically voters vote sincerely for most preferred candidates	Voters may either vote sincerely or strategically
Equilibrium issues	Equilibria depend on assumptions about voter preference configurations and issue space definitions and can be highly unlikely, typically when exist are unique	Often multiequilibria exist under general assumptions about voter preferences; likelihood of equilibria depend on coordination of voters in electoral coalitions

across parties after elections. Generally, our two major parties have dominated electoral coalition formation in U.S. politics. But what about the formation of electoral coalitions within the two major parties in choosing presidential candidates? How does the presidential primary process (whether front-loaded or drawn-out) affect the types of coalitions that form? And what about the coalition formation process in early and mail-in elections? Is it still likely to be dominated by the two major parties? These are issues that depend on the likelihood of voters choosing strategically and forming electoral coalitions, which we address.

Simultaneous Voting, Information, and Campaign Spending

In addition, of particular relevance to our concerns are the models of simultaneous voting when there is imperfect or incomplete information and models of voting where candidates use campaign expenditures to influence electoral outcomes. That is, policymakers worry about the advantages well-known and well-financed candidates may have in the virtual national primary when voting is essentially simultaneous. Therefore, it is useful to examine the existing theoretical literature on this situation. First we discuss models of simultaneous voting with information asymmetries without campaign contributions, and then we discuss models of voting with campaign contributions.

Juries and Elections

A number of researchers have considered how information asymmetries can affect the outcome of simultaneous voting using first-generation spatial voting models. Calvert 1986 reviews much of the early literature. Information can be imperfect or incomplete in elections in two major ways: candidates may be uncertain about voter preferences or voter choices in an election and/or voters may be uncertain about candidate positions on issues or ability to perform well in office.

Our interest is in the circumstances where voters have imperfect information about candidates. McKelvey and Ordeshook 1985, 1986 examine two-candidate elections where voters are in two groups: informed and uninformed. They show that given certain assumptions about the distribution of preferences, voter knowledge of these preferences, and the anticipated behavior of other voters, uninformed voters can act as if they are informed. That is, uninformed voters can use poll results and other information they have from informed voters to choose the candidate they would have chosen if they had been fully informed. Collier, Ordeshook, and Williams 1989 examine this prediction using experiments and find support for information aggregation.

Recently, academic study on information in voting has taken a different approach—examining the case where all are informed to some extent, but no one voter has complete information. These researchers have been especially interested in the Condorcet Jury Theorem (see, e.g., Austen-Smith and Banks 1996; Berg 1993; Condorcet 1785; Feddersen and Pesendofer 1996, 1998; Grofman and Feld 1988; Ladha 1992; McLennan 1998; Miller 1986; Young 1988). Condorcet argued that under certain conditions majority rule leads to outcomes that are desirable when voters have identical preferences but the information they have about the possible outcomes is asymmetrically distributed across the voters. For example, suppose that everyone on a jury agrees that if a criminal is guilty she should be convicted. However, voters have different pieces of information about the true state of the world (whether the criminal is guilty), and it is impossible for the voters to share this information. Condorcet contended that through majority voting, the choice of the voters as a group can be the "right" choice even when a randomly chosen individual voter's choice may not.

In terms of candidate competition, these models examine essentially the two-candidate case where voters' preferences over the candidates (if the voters had complete information) are all the same (Feddersen and Pesendorfer 1996, 1998 do consider the situation where there are other voters with different preferences). While this literature has provided useful insight into how the voting process can lead to information aggregation, it has not been extended, to our knowledge, to more than two candidates where there may not be a general consensus outcome if voters had complete information. Where consensus choices do not exist (e.g., in many three or more candidate races) and voters need to choose strategically to form electoral coalitions, then information asymmetries may have different types of effects. How information asymmetries affect the formation of electoral coalitions is an important question that we address.

Spending to Inform

The literature on information aggregation in majority rule does not consider how the information is distributed across voters, but takes the information distribution as a given. Most empirical studies of campaigns, as in Alvarez and Glasgow 1997, discussed in the previous chapter, conjecture that voters' information is provided via campaign advertising and the media. Others who have empirically and experimentally studied the relationship between voter information and campaign advertising are Alvarez 1997; Ansolabehere et. al. 1994; Brians and Wattenberg 1996; Faber and Storey 1984; Garramone 1984, 1985; Ivengar and Ansolabehere 1995; and Merritt 1984. Much of the empirical literature argues that the information distribution about candidates across voters is a function of the campaign spending of the candidates and is not exogenous.

Various first-generation spatial formal voting models have incorporated campaign spending. Much of this research, however, black-boxes the effect of spending on voter choices; it assumes that spending increases the probability that a candidate is elected without explicitly modeling the process (see Baron 1989a,b; Snyder 1991). Theorists who have attempted to get inside the black box have generally taken two approaches. One approach assumes that campaign spending provides voters with information about the candidates' policy positions, reducing the uncertainty voters have about their choices and thus affecting their preferences for candidates (see Austen-Smith 1987; Cameron and Enelow 1989; Hinich and Munger 1989; Simon 1998). The second major alternative approach assumes that campaign spending signals to voters non-policy related information about the candidates (like honesty or other character aspects) that contributors know about. Voters can just look at how much a candidate is spending and have some idea about what contributors think of the candidate. In these models, the advertisements financed by the campaign spending are themselves uninformative—they are just fluff (see Austen-Smith 1991;

Cameron and Jung 1990; Gerber 1996; Grossman and Helpman 1996; Potters, Sloof, and Van Winden 1997; Prat 1997).

Neither of these approaches is entirely satisfactory. The second approach belies the empirical evidence that voters do appear to learn policy information about candidates during electoral campaigns, while the first approach does not explain why candidates would reveal truthful information in campaign advertising or why voters would believe information provided by the candidates. In our model, we assume that voters have asymmetric information about the candidates and that this information is asymmetrically distributed because of both voter prior experience about the candidates and asymmetries in campaign advertising and media coverage. We assume that the information that voters have is truthful; that is, voters either do not know information about a candidate or have truthful information. In one sense, we are implicitly assuming that the media serves as a "truth police" on candidates so that information provided is accurate. Clearly, future research in this area is needed.

Modeling Sequence

Some voting models consider the sequential process that was typical of most of the post-1968 presidential primary contests and can occur in mail-in and early balloting. Generally, we can divide these models into two types: models centered on candidate or activist strategies that black-box voters and models focused on voter choices over a given set of candidates. First we will review the candidate or activist models and then discuss the voting models.

Candidates and Sequence

Aldrich 1980a and Abramowitz and Stone 1984 devise expected utility models of candidate entry and party activists respectively in presidential nomination contests. They look at how these actors make choices in order to maximize their expected satisfaction from the choices: the candidates or activists consider both their utility or satisfaction from various outcomes or events as well as the probability that these outcomes will occur in making their choices. Both find support for the expected utility explanation of the choices of candidates and party activists. As discussed in chapter 2, we also use expected utility maximization in our model. These models examine the choices of the candidates or party activists in a decision-theoretic framework, that is, taking the choices of the other actors as givens.

An important focus of dynamic work on candidates in presidential primaries is the role of momentum. Aldrich 1980b presents a formal model that captures the dynamics of momentum. In that model, campaign resources that candidates invest in a state affect their probability of success in that state. When candidates do better than expected, their probability in later states is positively affected and vice versa. Aldrich does not provide a micro-level basis for the determination of the probabilities of success in the primaries. We have already discussed a possible micro-level explanation for momentum from the empirical studies of voter information levels during the 1976, 1980, and 1984 presidential nomination contests. The conjecture typically made is that as the primaries progress, media coverage of the outcomes of the early primaries and the candidates as well as campaign advertising provide voters with information, which affects their preferences over the candidates. Brady and Ansolabehere 1989 and Bartels 1988 discuss the emphasis in the news media on the early caucuses and primaries and the extent to which this information affects voters.

Given the dynamics of momentum, most studies of candidate strategy have accentuated the importance of candidate entry in early contests and the influence of early voters. In contrast to this stress on momentum, Strumpf 1997 suggests that it is possible for the sequential voting process to actually benefit candidates who are supported more by later voters than earlier voters. He models the sequential voting process as a war of attrition between two candidates whose probability of success in a set of states varies across the states. In his model, as in Aldrich's and others', voters are black-boxed, represented by probabilities of success for the candidates that are subject to random influences. That is, candidates know that they may have more supporters in a later state than an early state, but there is uncertainty as to the size of that support. If a candidate has early success when it is unexpected, she is more likely to win the nomination than when her early success (or especially failure) is expected. This is because an early, unexpected win is an extra success on top of the success she expects to have in the later elections. Strumpf suggests that this strategic effect benefits candidates who are preferred by later voters.

Nevertheless, as noted above, Strumpf's model does not explicitly explore voter choices in the dynamic contests but focuses instead on candidate strategic behavior. The uncertainty in the model is a random effect on voter preferences that is unaffected by the dynamics of the campaign or candidate behavior. The most interesting aspect of Strumpf's analysis is that despite the fact that there can be advantages to the candidates who are preferred by later voters, the causal empirical evidence of front-loading by states shows that this strategic effect is not empirically significant enough to induce states to be satisfied with later primary dates. This suggests that voter choices in later states are influenced by the outcomes of earlier states, unlike the assumption in Strumpf's analysis.

The predictions of models of candidate competition in the sequential voting process, then, depend crucially on the assumptions a researcher makes about the effects of sequence on voter choices. In Aldrich 1980b voter choices are assumed to be influenced by the results of earlier contests and by campaign expenditures. Why they are so influenced is not explicitly modeled. The model predicts that early victories can have significant effects on which candidates win because of the influence. In Strumpf 1997, in contrast, later voter choices are independent of the choices made by earlier voters but subject to random influences. Again, voter choices are not explicitly modeled. His model predicts that later voters may be influential in determining which candidates win. In order to fully understand which macro-level model works we need to understand the micro-level dynamics of voters in sequential voting situations.

Voters and Sequence

Despite the fact that the representativeness of early voters in sequential voting and whether voting is sequential or simultaneous appear to matter substantially to policymakers in presidential primaries and in mail-in and early balloting, there is very little theoretical analysis comparing the voting systems as a whole. Most formal models of voting examine simultaneous voting, where all decisions are made at once.

There are some game-theoretic models of sequential voting. In game theory the actors make strategic choices; they make choices recognizing that their expected satisfaction depends on their expectations and perceptions of the strategies of other actors *and* recognizing that the choices of other actors are also dependent. Assuming perfect information, Sloth (1993) shows that the subgame perfect equilibria of roll-call voting games (in which voters vote one after another) are closely related to sophisticated equilibria of agenda voting games where one voter has control over the agenda (sequence of alternatives) and voters vote simultaneously. Subgame-perfect equilibria are outcomes in a sequential game in which the strategies are also optimal in each subgame or part of the sequential game. In a sequential voting game, subgame-perfect strategies of voters are ones such that the choice of each voter is optimal when he or she makes it. Thus, Sloth's work shows that the outcomes of sequential voting under perfect information are like the outcomes of voting where one voter has control over an agenda. But this analysis does not yield much insight into a comparison of the two systems when voters' information about the alternatives is less than perfect.[4]

Closer to our research is the work of Fey (1996), Witt (1997), and Dekel and Piccione (1997), who examine sequential voting games in the spirit of recent work in the economics literature on information cascades. The economics literature examines the case where consumers have incomplete information and use inferences based on purchases of other consumers to judge the quality of a product. An information cascade occurs when consumers ignore information they independently have to follow the lead of others. Economists have argued that these models can explain things like fads and crazes for certain products that seem irrational. Fey and Witt show that since sequential voting involves a collective decision, voting cascades are not perfect Bayesian equilibria. That is, it is not optimal for voters to ignore their own information in sequential voting games.[5] Our work is distinct from Fey's and Witt's in that they consider an electoral situation in which voters have identical preferences over the outcomes and only differ in the information they have on the state of the world. In our model, we appraise the case where voters differ both in the information they have and their preferences over the outcomes.

Dekel and Piccione (1997) assess sequential voting with two candidates where voters do not have common preferences. They show that informative equilibria of a similar simultaneous voting game over two choices (equilibria when the outcome uses all the information about candidates) are also equilibria in sequential voting elections. In our model we examine voting over three options rather than two; we purposely choose a voting case where there are multiple equilibria under complete information (like in the Goodell, Ottinger, and Buckley New York senate race) in order to examine the effect of voting structure on the likelihood of the various equilibria. That is, we are able to consider how likely it is that voters will vote strategically and form electoral coalitions and how sequential voting may affect that likelihood in races with more than two candidates.

Our Model

In the next chapter, we present our basic voting model and theoretical predictions. In our model we make assumptions about the distribution of information in simultaneous voting that we believe capture the realities of the virtual national primary as compared with sequential voting in drawn-out primaries. Our assumptions also are made to highlight the concerns of policymakers about mail-in and early balloting as compared with traditional one-day elections. Our focus is on voter choices and how the two different electoral processes and the way information is distributed in these processes affect these choices and the types of candidates selected. We investigate the extent voters choose strategically and form electoral coalitions under the two electoral processes.

In our experimental design, discussed in chapters 6 and 7, we vary the representativeness of early voters in the sequential voting elections. Hence, we can consider the concern of whether front-loading lessens the ability of voters to gain information during the nomination process as compared with the concern that in drawn-out primaries nonrepresentative voters can have a disproportionate influence on the outcome. We can evaluate whether early nonrepresentative voters in mail-in and early balloting systems can have an undue influence.

We do not examine candidate strategic behavior, either in terms of candidate entry and exit choices or in providing voters with information. We do not explicitly incorporate in our model campaign spending or the news media. While we think these aspects of presidential primaries and other elections are important and should be studied, we believe that a good first step is to understand voter choices in simultaneous and sequential voting environments well. We hope that our research can be useful for future work that considers these aspects of presidential primaries and other elections that we ignore in our simple model.

CHAPTER 5

Our Voting Story

In this chapter, we present a stylized three-candidate election story. In our story, each of the three candidates has a group of supporters (like Goodell, Ottinger, and Buckley), and no candidate has enough supporters to be a first choice of the majority of the voters—which we believe highlights the dilemmas faced when voters try to form electoral coalitions. We use our story (or model) to analyze both simultaneous voting as in the virtual national primary and other elections where voting is simultaneous and sequential voting as in drawn-out primaries and mail-in and early balloting.[1] Our model is based on Myerson and Weber 1993. A technical presentation of the model and our theoretical predictions is provided in appendix B (see also Morton and Williams 1999). Our model is a second-generation voting model, as described in the preceding chapter. As noted in chapter 1, our model is simple, designed to capture what we believe are the salient characteristics of the voting processes in primaries, mail-in and early balloting, and single-day elections.

Assumptions about Voters and Candidates

In our model, we assume that simple plurality-rule voting takes place with three candidates. That is, we assume that the candidate that receives the most votes wins; we do not impose a majority requirement where the winner must receive a certain percentage of the vote or face a runoff election.[2] We assume that there are three types of voters: liberals, moderates, and conservatives. We also assume that each group of voters has a favorite candidate, and so there are three candidates: a liberal, a moderate, and a conservative.

We use the concept of utility to describe the voters' preferences over the candidates. That is, a voter's utility from a particular candidate represents what the voter receives if that candidate is elected. This could be something tangible like a particular public policy or intangible like a personal satisfaction from having a candidate elected who is from one's own region or religion. There is nothing in our model that assumes that voters are selfish; they could prefer one candidate to another for altruistic reasons.[3]

Voters' utility from candidates is described in table 5.1. Liberal voters most

TABLE 5.1. Voter Utility Matrix ($1 > \alpha > 1/16$)

Voter Types	Candidates		
	Liberal	Moderate	Conservative
Liberal voters	1	α	0
Moderate voters	α	1	α
Conservative voters	0	α	1

prefer the liberal candidate, their second preference is the moderate, and their third is the conservative; moderate voters most prefer the moderate candidate, and are indifferent between the liberal and conservative candidates; and conservative voters most prefer the conservative candidate, their second choice is the moderate, and their third is the liberal. Furthermore, we assume that the utility each type of voter receives from his or her second preference is equal to α. Alternatively we could assume that α is voter-specific, that is, that voter i's utility from their second preference is given by α_i, with predictions comparable to those presented here. We assume that $1 > \alpha > \frac{1}{16}$.

We measure risk aversion in liberal and conservative voters by α. That is, it measures how much a voter is willing to take a "sure win" of his or her second preferred candidate to a lottery over his or her first and least preferred candidates. For example, suppose that in a two-way contest between the liberal and conservative candidates, the probability that the liberal candidate will win is equal to $\frac{2}{3}$. Then, if $\alpha = \frac{2}{3}$, liberal voters are indifferent between this two-way contest or lottery and a sure win by the moderate candidate. The expected utility for liberal voters from the lottery or contest between the liberal and conservative candidates is equal to the utility from the sure win by the moderate. That is:

$$\text{Expected Utility} = (\tfrac{2}{3}) \times [\text{Utility from liberal candidate}]$$

$$+ (\tfrac{1}{3}) \times [\text{Utility from conservative candidate}]$$

$$= (\tfrac{2}{3}) \times 1 + (\tfrac{1}{3}) \times 0 = \tfrac{2}{3}$$

If $\alpha > \frac{2}{3}$, liberal voters will prefer the sure win by the moderate to the lottery between the liberal and conservative candidates, and if $\alpha < \frac{2}{3}$, liberal voters will prefer the lottery. As α decreases, liberal voters, therefore, are more willing to accept riskier lotteries between the liberal and conservative candidates (where the probability that their preferred candidate, the liberal, will win is lower) than a sure win by the moderate. Similarly, α measures risk aversion in conservative voters.

For moderate voters, however, they have only a first and last preference,

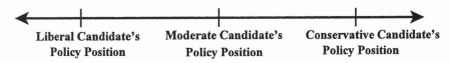

Liberal Candidate's   **Moderate Candidate's**   **Conservative Candidate's**
Policy Position   **Policy Position**   **Policy Position**

Fig. 5.1.   Candidates aligned in a single-dimensional issue space

and α does not have the same meaning. These voters, regardless of risk aversion, should always prefer to vote for the moderate candidate and should only vote for the liberal or conservative candidates by mistake. Thus, for these voters, α measures the cost of a mistake. When α is high, mistakes are less costly for moderate voters.

One way to conceptualize the preferences the voters have for the candidates is that the candidates have positions in an ideological dimension or dimensions and voters' utility over the ideological dimension induces their preference orderings over the candidates (as our titles of the voters and candidates suggest). Candidate policy positions under this conceptualization are shown in figure 5.1. Voters can be assumed to have single-peaked preferences with ideal points at their most preferred candidates' policy positions, as in figure 4.1. That is, moderate voters' most preferred policy position is at the moderate candidate's policy position; as policy moves away from the moderate's position, moderate voters' utility falls. Similarly, liberal voters' most preferred policy position is at the liberal candidate's policy position, and conservative voters' most preferred policy position is at the conservative candidate's policy position.

But our analysis is not restricted to a one-dimensional issue space. If the election is the nomination of a candidate for a later general election, then voter preferences may reflect voters' subjective expected utility from the general election, incorporating the probabilities that a candidate will win the general election along with the candidate's policy position. The preferences may also reflect nonideological differences between the candidates that voters care about. Some empirical research on voter choices in presidential primaries argue that candidate qualities are more important factors than ideology and issues (Stone, Rappoport, and Atkeson 1995; Geer 1989; Marshall 1981; Williams et al. 1976). We use the terms *liberal, moderate,* and *conservative,* but the underlying policy space may be multidimensional instead of one-dimensional, or the preferences may be derived from nonpolicy differences between the candidates. We use the labels of *liberal, moderate,* and *conservative* primarily to ease exposition, but our analysis is not restricted to this conceptualization.

We assume that the numbers of each type of voters are such that no type is in a clear majority, that is, each group has less than 50 percent of the voters. We also assume that the numbers of liberals and conservatives are equal, and greater than the number of moderate voters. Notice that the sum of total voter utility is greater when the candidate elected is the moderate than when the liberal or conservative candidate is elected. Suppose that there are 10 liberal voters, 4 moderate voters, and 10 conservative voters. If the moderate wins, the sum of voter utility for all voters equals $4 + 20\alpha$, and if the liberal or conservative win, the sum of voter utility equals $5 + 4\alpha$. Since $\alpha > \frac{1}{16}$, then the sum when the moderate wins is greater than the sum when either the liberal or conservative wins. Thus, the moderate is the candidate that gives the most total utility to all voters.

Voters are allowed to choose only one candidate. Note that we do not allow for abstention in our analysis. Abstention in sequential voting is of interest, of course, particularly when later voters may choose not to vote if they think that early balloting has determined the outcome as in Western states in presidential elections. We plan to expand the model to allow for abstention in future analyses.

Our simple model focuses on a case in which there is a single candidate who will defeat any other candidate in a pairwise competition, but is the first preference of only a minority of voters (will not win in a three-way race if all voters choose sincerely their first preference). The moderate is this candidate, also called the Condorcet winner (see Condorcet 1785). In a three-way contest, for the moderate to win some liberals and conservatives must choose strategically for their second preference. They must join an electoral coalition with moderate voters. We might also call the moderate the candidate preferred by the "median voter" in the electorate. In other words, if the candidates are aligned in one-dimensional issue space as in figure 5.1, and moderates' ideal points are equal to the moderate's position, the moderate voters' ideal point is the median ideal point in the electorate. We have also already seen that the moderate candidate maximizes the sum of voter utility. Relaxing the assumption of equality of the proportion of liberals and conservatives does not change qualitatively the results that follow as long as each is greater than the number of moderates.

Clearly, there is a wide range of different assumptions that we could make about voter preferences over the candidates. We chose our preference configuration because we wanted to concentrate on the case where there are significant differences in voter preferences, and no candidate has a clear mandate or is the first preference of the majority of the electorate even if voters have complete information about the candidates (like in the Goodell, Ottinger, and Buckley contest in 1970, discussed in chap. 4). In complete information simultaneous voting, as discussed below, there are election outcomes in which any of the three candidates could win. Thus our analysis is different from the approach taken by others who have looked at sequential voting under incomplete information, such as Fey 1996 and Witt 1997, where if voters did have complete information, they would agree on a candidate and complete information voting is straightforward, or as in Dekel and Piccione 1997, where voters may have different preferences, but under complete information there would be a clear winner. Our model is able to explore how the representativeness of early voters' preferences may affect the electoral outcome (which candidate wins in actuality) and choices of later voters in sequential voting.

The Importance of the Likelihood of Close Races

How We Model Voters' Choices

When voters choose in two-candidate races their choices are straightforward. If Buckley, for example, had faced only Goodell in 1970, liberal voters in New York would have easily known who they wanted to choose. However, when there are more than two candidates, voter choices are complex, and voters need to consider not only which candidate they prefer, but also the candidates' chances of winning. Even more important, they need to consider how best to use their vote. Which candidates do they expect to be in a close race for first place in the election? Do they think it is likely to be a race between Buckley and Goodell with Ottinger having very little chance of winning? If so, then even a voter who prefers Ottinger for a first choice may find it optimal to vote for Goodell. And Goodell and Buckley supporters will sincerely choose their first preferences. If voters had had these expectations in 1970, maybe Goodell would have defeated Buckley.

But perhaps voters think that both Goodell and Ottinger are equally likely to be in a close race for first place with Buckley—that neither has an advantage over Buckley. In that case, Ottinger supporters may find it optimal to vote sincerely for their first preference, just like Goodell and Buckley supporters, leading to an election where all three candidates receive votes from their supporters and all three have some chance of winning, even the Condorcet loser, Buckley. Myerson and Weber (1993) argue that outcomes like Buckley's win can be explained by these types of voter expectations.

Following Myerson and Weber we assume that how a voter then perceives the relative likelihood of the assorted "close races" matters in ballot choices. Still we need to make some additional assumptions about voters and their expectations. Our assumptions are:

1. Near-ties between two candidates are perceived to be much more likely than between three or more candidates.
2. A voter's perceived probability that a particular ballot changes the outcome of the election between candidates is proportional to the difference in the votes cast for the two candidates. We call these probabili-

ties the pivot probabilities that two candidates are in a close race for first place.

3. Voters make ballot choices in order to maximize their expected utility from the outcome of the election.

Gains and Losses versus Expected Gains and Expected Losses

As discussed in appendix B, Myerson and Weber show that a voter will vote in order to maximize a weighted sum of the voter's utility differences between the candidates. That is, voters will evaluate each candidate choice by comparing the utility gained or lost by choosing one of the other candidates as compared to that choice. For example, consider a liberal voter. The gain in utility to the liberal voter from choosing the liberal candidate instead of the conservative is equal to 1, her gain from choosing the liberal instead of the moderate is equal to $1 - \alpha$. In contrast, if she chooses the moderate candidate, her loss from choosing that candidate as compared to the liberal is $\alpha - 1$, but she still gains utility from choosing the moderate over the conservative, that is, she gains α.

But voters do not look just at the sum of the losses and gains across candidates. If they did so, they would always vote sincerely for their first preferences because choosing their first preference will always yield the highest gain. They weight these losses and gains by the likelihood that the election will be a close race between the two candidates compared (the pivot probabilities). Consider the liberal voter who thinks that the election is likely to be a close race between the conservative and moderate candidates and that the liberal candidate has very little chance of winning. The liberal voter will put a zero weight (zero pivot probability) on the gains of voting for the liberal candidate as compared to either the conservative or moderate candidates. The expected utility of voting for the liberal candidate for the liberal voter, under these expectations, is equal to zero, since the gains are not expected to occur.

Conversely, the weight on the gain from voting for the moderate candidate as compared to the conservative is positive (positive pivot probability), since the liberal voter perceives that there is a likelihood of a close race between these two. So for this voter, the expected utility of voting of choosing the moderate candidate is positive, and greater than the expected utility of voting of choosing the liberal candidate. This voter will find it optimal to vote strategically for her second preference, forming an electoral coalition with moderate voters. Naturally, the liberal voter would never vote for the conservative candidate, since her expected utility from voting for him is always either zero or negative. Notice also that moderate voters always choose the moderate candidate, since their expected utility from voting for either the liberal or conservative candidates is likewise always either zero or negative.

What happens when a liberal voter thinks that both the liberal and moderate candidates are likely to be in a close race for first place with the conservative candidate (the pivot probabilities of these two close races are both positive and roughly equal)? In this case, liberal voters will receive a higher expected utility from voting for the liberal candidate than the moderate and will vote sincerely for the liberal candidate.

Likelihood of Close Races and Expected Election Outcomes

The pivot probabilities, or perceived likelihood of close races, are then as important for understanding voter choices as the gains and losses in utility from those choices. What determines these pivot probabilities? Myerson and Weber (1993) show that voters will place a positive weight on the utility gained or lost from voting for candidates that are: (1) expected to be in first place alone; (2) in a tie for first place; or (3) in second place when there is an expected unique first place winner. Voters perceive that their choices may affect the outcome of the election in these cases.

Assuming that voters place a positive weight on the utility difference for voting for the second place candidate when there is an expected unique first place winner does not necessarily mean that the voters perceive that the relevant pivot probability that these two candidates are in a close race is large. That is, the expected difference between the expected first and second place finishers may be great. The assumption is only that the pivot probability is positive although it may be extremely small, almost negligible, as pivot probabilities might be in a large presidential primary. Our assumption is simply that voters consider which candidates might potentially be in close races for first place in making their decisions, knowing that the probability of such a close race might be extremely tiny. Voters choose the candidate for whom their expected utility gain is highest given their expectations of the outcome.

Although the pivot probabilities can be extremely small for our analysis to hold, some may question the assumption that they are positive at all in large elections such as presidential primaries. If voters perceived all the pivot probabilities as equal to zero then they would choose either sincerely for their most preferred candidates or based purely on other, nonstrategic, motivations. However, empirical evidence suggests that voters do choose strategically. Abramson, Aldrich, and Rohde (1998) find indications of strategic voting in three-candidate U.S. presidential contests. Ideally, an experimental study with a larger number of subjects might address the issue of the extent that voters consider strategic concerns in large elections more directly, but it is not possible given current budget constraints on experimental research. One way to increase the sample size is to conduct experiments over the Internet (see McGraw, Morton, and Williams forthcoming, for a discussion of these).[4]

Sincere versus Strategic Voting Equilibria

In solving a formal model, researchers look for equilibria or solutions. Voting equilibria exist when voter perceptions of relatively close races are justified by the electoral outcome. In our analysis, we restrict ourselves to symmetric equilibria, that is, equilibria in which identical voters have identical strategies. This is standard in models of large elections. Essentially, voters' strategies are functions of their preferences, and symmetry implies that the relationship between preference and strategy is identical across voters. We assume that no voter knowingly chooses her least preferred candidate. That is, voting for her least preferred candidate will never increase her payoffs.

Suppose that the voters are choosing simultaneously and have perfect information about the candidates. The interesting question is, When will liberals and conservatives choose strategically for their second preference, the moderate candidate, or sincerely for their first, the liberal and conservative candidates, respectively? When will liberals and conservatives form electoral coalitions with moderates? In a voting game where there is complete information under our assumptions on voter preferences, equilibria are possible in which the moderate wins (liberals or conservatives choose him strategically) or the liberal and conservative candidates tie (liberals and conservatives choose their first choices sincerely). Notice that we would never expect both liberals and conservatives to choose strategically the moderate because then both are equally likely (or unlikely) to be in a close race with the moderate, and neither liberals nor conservatives would be maximizing their expected utility. So there are three possible equilibria and two types of equilibria—one where all voters choose sincerely and the liberal and conservative candidates tie, and two where one type of extremists choose strategically the moderate and the moderate wins. Both types of equilibria are possible. We call the first type *sincere voting equilibria* and the second type *strategic voting equilibria.*

Which equilibrium occurs in actuality is determined, then, by voter expectations. When a liberal or conservative voter perceives that her most preferred candidate, the liberal or conservative, respectively, is likely to be in last place, it is optimal for her to choose strategically helping the moderate to win, and, in equilibrium, the outcome justifies her expectations. When a liberal or conservative voter perceives that her most preferred candidate is more or equally likely to be in a close race for first place, she will choose sincerely her first preference, helping her favorite to be in a close race for first place and also justifying her expectations.

Although the moderate is the preference of the median voter, the Condorcet winner, and the candidate who maximizes the sum of utility for all voters, he does not necessarily win in all equilibria since voter expectations about the electoral outcome and likely close races can result in the moderate losing.

Voter expectations that the moderate will lose can become a self-fulfilling prophecy. By choosing this distribution of voter preferences over candidates we can investigate theoretically and empirically how the different voting systems (simultaneous and sequential) affect which equilibrium occurs, the likelihood of electoral coalition formation, and how information asymmetries work in an election where there are possible multiple equilibrium outcomes.

Modeling Information Asymmetries and Simultaneous versus Sequential Voting

Why Information Variation Is Important

We are particularly interested in the effects of simultaneous (like in the virtual national primary) versus sequential voting (as in drawn-out primaries and early and mail-in balloting) and the representativeness of early voters in sequential voting under incomplete voter information about candidates. As we noted in chapter 1, policymakers argue that when voting is drawn-out (sequential), voters are able to make more informed choices about candidates and the electoral outcomes will be different. When voting is compacted (simultaneous), policymakers argue that candidates well-known to all voters are advantaged and more likely to win.

Candidates already well-known have an advantage both in that their names are already recognizable and they can more easily raise financial resources. Shapiro comments: "Front-loading all the major primaries in March eliminates what in political lingo is called the 'reload factor.' That is the ability of an underdog candidate to pay for a national campaign with the money and the media attention that he garners from a dramatic finish in New Hampshire. Just two weeks after Pat Buchanan (admittedly not exactly the model for political reform) confounded the experts in New Hampshire, he was overwhelmed by Dole's bankroll and effectively out of the race" (1997). Rhodes Cooks reports: "The current system is tailor-made for 'someone who is well-known and well-financed and can compete in 35 states in 28 days,' says Mark Siegel, who was executive director of the DNC in the mid-1970s. 'Only one man can do that: Al Gore. This system is really made to order for him'" (1997, p. 1942).

Policymakers also worry that in mail-in and early balloting systems early voters would have different information from election day ones and that early voters will make choices different from what they would make if they had chosen on election day. Early voters may also be unrepresentative of the electorate in mail-in and early balloting and may have a disproportionate influence on the electoral outcome as well.

How Information Varies across Voting Systems

In other formal models of sequential voting under incomplete information voters all have some information about the choices but the information differs across voters. The question that concerns these researchers is how voters might aggregate this information through the sequential process and whether, when compared to simultaneous voting, the outcomes are different (more or less close to the outcomes that would result if voters are "informed"). The theories compare two hypothetical voting systems under the same information conditions.

However, in naturally occurring presidential primaries, information is distributed differently in the two voting systems (front-loaded versus drawn-out primaries). That is, when primaries are compacted (simultaneous voting), candidates campaign virtually nationally at once and voters are exposed to similar information about the candidates. They do have incomplete information, but the asymmetry is not as much across voters as it is across candidates. That is, well-financed front-runners are much better known to voters than the other candidates are when voting is simultaneous (primaries are front-loaded). Dole and Gore are examples of the candidates voters would know well. This is also likely to be true in elections held on a single day.

In contrast, when primaries have been drawn-out (sequential voting), not all voters have the same information about the candidates since candidates do not all campaign nationally at the same time. The asymmetry across voters is important. Voters in different states had information about distinct candidates when they vote when primaries were more drawn-out. Aldrich 1980b, in his study of candidate choices, shows how candidates often campaign unequally across states, which affects voter information levels in the primaries. Because candidates typically have held other political offices such as senator, representative, or governor, the constituents they have formerly had and their neighboring states are likely to know these candidates better than others. Note that we are not denying that there may be asymmetries in information across voters as well in simultaneous voting elections. Our contention is that there is *more* asymmetry across voters in sequential than in simultaneous voting elections.

Similar comparisons are true for comparing mail-in and early balloting with elections that are held on a single day. In mail-in and early balloting, voters who choose earlier have different types of information about candidates than voters who choose later. Later voters may also have information on the outcome of early balloting as well. But when all voters choose at the same time, voters are likely to have similar information about the candidates, although it may be unequally distributed across candidates. Table 5.2 summarizes the information differences.

TABLE 5.2.   Voting Sequence and Information Distributions

Types of Voter Knowledge	Simultaneous Voting Elections (Frontloaded Primaries, Traditional Single Day Elections)	Sequential Voting Elections (Drawn Out Primaries, Elections with Mail-in and Early Voting)
Voter knowledge of candidates across voters	Voters generally have the same knowledge about candidates	Early and late voters have different types of knowledge about candidates
Voter knowledge of candidates across candidates	Voters generally know more about some candidates than about others, i.e., some candidates are well-known	
Voter knowledge of other voter decisions	Voters do not know how other voters have voted	Late voters may have some knowledge of how early voters have voted

Information Asymmetries in Our Model: Simultaneous Voting Elections

Given our analysis, in our model we assume that voters in simultaneous voting elections know only the policy position of one of the candidates and have less knowledge about the other two candidates. For example, voters may know that the liberal candidate is a liberal but not know which of the other two candidates is the moderate and which is the conservative. We assume that they know that neither is liberal. Alternatively, voters may know which one is the conservative but not know which is the liberal or which is the moderate (again we assume that they know that neither is conservative). This situation is designed to represent the case where balloting is compact as in front-loaded primaries or elections held on a single day and candidates campaign to all voters at the same time. However, one candidate is better known than the rest of the candidates when the voters choose (like George W. Bush in the Republican primaries in 2000 or Albert Gore in the Democratic primaries in 2000).

Information Asymmetries in Our Model: Sequential Voting Elections

We assume that in sequential voting elections, voter knowledge of the candidates depends on whether a voter chooses early or late. In our model of sequential voting elections, we divide the voters into two equal groups, early and later voters. Each group is assumed, like in simultaneous voting elections above, to know the identity of one candidate but not the other two. However, later voters also know something else. They know the outcome of earlier choices. We consider the effects of two types of horse-race information. We consider the effects of horse-race information when later voters know the outcome of early choices by voter type—how liberals, conservatives, and moderates chose (*high information*)—and when later voters only know the total outcome of early balloting (*low information*).

We can think of the early group as voters in a state that has its primary election first, such as New Hampshire. These voters are assumed to gain information about the distribution of candidates in the primary during the campaign process, but the information is unequal in the sense that more information is revealed about one candidate than the other two. The later voters are then in a state that has its primary subsequently after the results of the choices in New Hampshire are publicly known. This later group also is assumed to acquire information about the distribution of candidates during the campaign process in a similar unequal sense, but with more information on a different candidate. This can happen either because the voters know more about different candidates before the election process begins or because candidates strategically campaign differently in different states when primaries are drawn-out as discussed in Aldrich 1980b. Later state voters also have information on the choices in early states (horse-race information).

In mail-in and early balloting systems it is also probable that early and later voters have different types of information about the candidates, as discussed in chapters 1 and 3. Later voters may also have some information about how early voters have chosen from poll results, although the low information case may more accurately reflect the information they would have.

Hence, later voters in the sequential voting elections receive two types of information: early voter choices and specific information they have on one of the candidates. If the early balloting reveals the information early voters have, later voters will be fully informed about the true distribution of candidates (i.e., they will know the policy positions of two of the three candidates and therefore be able to infer the position of the third). In the sequential voting elections, then, early voters use primarily differences between the candidates they learn during the campaign (but they do not have complete information) in making their decisions, while later voters use both candidate differences they learn during the campaign and horse-race aspects of previous primaries to infer additional information. There is empirical evidence that voters do learn during the presidential primary process (as reviewed in chap. 2). While Keeter and Zukin 1983 do not find significant differences, Alvarez and Glasgow 1997, Bartels 1988, and Popkin 1991 find evidence of such learning.

Justifications for Our Assumptions

Clearly our choice to model later voters as receiving only horse-race information from early balloting (rather than the same information that early voters have) and the identity of a different candidate from that known to early voters (not information specifically about the front-runner in early choices) is just one possible way to represent the information process of sequential voting in presidential primaries or other sequential voting elections. We chose to model the information in this fashion for the following two reasons:

1. We assume that later voters have independent information in sequential voting but that all voters have common information in simultaneous voting.

There is evidence that voters in different states choosing at different times know distinct things about the distribution of candidates in presidential primaries. Moreover, the nature of sequential voting in presidential primaries implies that it is unreasonable to assume that voters in later states have the same information about candidates as voters in early states (as we do in simultaneous voting). That is, as campaigns progress, events occur that alter the focus of campaign reporting and campaigns. There is also evidence that later voters know, because of the publicity given early balloting, that early voters received different information about the distribution of candidates than later voters, information that later voters cannot acquire because the campaign processes in the states are different.

Consider the comments of the secretary of state of California in the May 6, 1996, *Los Angeles Times:*

> Earlier this year residents of a small New England state with a population roughly equivalent to that of California's Alameda County were able to eat breakfast, share war stories and then intimately discuss the future of America one-on-one with a number of prominent presidential candidates. On Feb. 20, the nation watched as New Hampshire voters played a major role in determining who would be the nominees for president. Why New Hampshire? Why not Alameda County? Each has about 1.5 million residents and 700,000 registered voters. It can be argued that Alameda County, with its three professional sports franchises, world class university and major international port adds more to America's gross national product than several entire states.

When voting is sequential, the campaigning in primaries differs by state. As Palmer discusses, the campaigning in New Hampshire and Iowa is a type of "retail politics," and candidates who use the large-scale approach appropriate in simultaneous voting or as used in later states are actually disadvantaged: "New Hampshire is as susceptible as any other state in the union to the convenience of wholesale, media-driven politicking, but this campaign technique, which pays dividends in New York or California, is less effective in the Granite State, as the failure of the Forbes media blitz in 1996 demonstrated" (1997, 53–54). Thus, the assumption that in sequential voting the distribution of information across voters by when they choose is different as compared with simultaneous voting is essential for determining whether the two systems as actually used have different effects.

Similarly, when elections have mail-in and early voting, candidates are likely to conduct separate campaigns as discussed in chapter 3. Early voters are more likely to be partisans (voters with strong party ties) and thus are more likely to have different types of information about candidates than later voters who are more likely to be independents and not as strongly motivated by partisan concerns. For example, Palfrey and Poole (1987) find that voter information about candidates is a function of their ideological positions. Although the time difference between when early and mail-in voters choose may be argued to be not huge, in smaller elections it can result in candidates engaging in distinctly different campaigns to distinct groups of voters.

An alternative approach to the one we take would have the information distribution the same across voting systems (either assuming that voters in the sequential voting elections have all the same information as in the simultaneous voting elections or assuming voters in the simultaneous voting elections have different information about the candidates by groups as in the sequential voting elections). Our model results in an experimental design (discussed in more detail in chapter 6) that, in this respect, using Roth's terminology, "Whispers in the Ears of Princes" more than it "Speaks to Theorists" (1995, 22). That is, according to Roth, experiments that "Speak to Theorists" are ones "designed to test the predictions of well articulated formal theories, and to observe unpredicted regularities, in a controlled environment that allows these observations to be unambiguously interpreted in relationship to the theory. Such experiments are intended to feed back into the theoretical literature—i.e., they are part of a dialogue between experimenters and theorists." An experiment that "Whispers in the Ears of Princes" "deals with the dialogue between experimenters and policy makers. . . . Their characteristic feature is that the experimental environment is designed to closely resemble, in certain respects, the naturally occurring environment that is the focus of interest for the policy purpose at hand." Holding the information distribution constant and only changing the voting process is a model and experimental design that would provide useful information about the effect of one variable, the change in the voting process, whereas we vary both the voting process and the distribution of information in order to capture more closely an important aspect of the naturally occurring environment (that information distribution does vary with the voting process).

> 2. We assume that later voters have horse-race information about early balloting.

The media coverage of the balloting in early states is primarily focused on horse-race information. For discussions of media concentration on horse races during presidential primaries see Patterson 1980 and Robinson and Sheehan 1983. As Palmer observes:

> Reporters can be too easily drawn into discussions of which candidates are ahead, which are behind, which are moving up or falling back, to the detriment of serious, considered reporting of policy debates. . . . Factors such as advertising revenue, audience totals and changing perspectives on the presentation and development of political stories inevitably affect media approaches to election coverage. The late NBC News' senior political commentator, John Chancellor, regretted the horse race aspects but added in the media's defense that it becomes very difficult for editors and television producers to avoid them in the early caucuses and primaries since so many candidates are in the running. (1997, 102)

But horse-race information is not simply who won early primaries. In sequential voting the media reports more than just which candidate is the frontrunner, but the relative size of the candidates' victories. Again, Palmer comments: "In presidential primaries, and in New Hampshire above all, victories can be qualified. A first-place finish can prove insufficient, and a close second can sometimes be represented as a moral victory overshadowing the achievement of the winner" (1997, 102). Hence, it is not just whether a candidate won or not that is reported, but the size of the victory. The perceived winner of a primary is not always the actual winner—Palmer notes that in four out of the 12 Democratic presidential primaries in New Hampshire from 1952 to 1996 the perceived winner was different from the actual winner. In 1968, Johnson won and McCarthy was the perceived winner, Muskie won in 1972 while McGovern was the perceived winner, in 1988 Dukakis won but the perceived winner was inconclusive since Dukakis's victory was interpreted by the media as establishing him only as one among three front-runners, and in 1992 Tsongas won but Clinton was the perceived winner. We wished to determine if voters used the horse-race information that is provided about early voting to infer information about the candidates that they did not have. If we assume that later voters have the same information that early voters have we would have been unable to determine how much later voters use horse-race information in their vote choice.

Currently there is little evidence that in early and mail-in balloting later voters are provided with information about early voting outcomes. However, it would be premature to conclude that this information will not be provided to later voters. Public opinion polls are conducted during the early voting period, and voters are asked whether they voted or not. The incentive to gather and report the results from early voting will no doubt be strong if the use of early voting increases as the quote from the news executive in chapter 1 suggests. Our results speak to whether such reporting will be problematic—whether it will have effects on electoral outcomes and later voter behavior.

As noted above, we varied the extent that we assumed later voters knew the horse-race information by early voter type. While assuming voters know the breakdown of early choices by types may seem at first glance unrealistic, many public reports on elections outcomes are typically broken down by groups of voters. For example, newspapers and television stories often focus on how blacks or women choose, how union members choose, and how votes are distributed by income groups. Thus, we feel it is reasonable to assume that voters may know more than just who won in an election but how different large groups of voters actually chose. In order to evaluate whether the more detailed information was particularly useful for voters, however, we considered both cases where later voters knew detailed information about early choices and when they only knew aggregate outcomes.

An alternative model would have assumed that later voters always know about the front-runner in early balloting. However, that approach would, in many cases, have prevented us from determining whether later voters used the horse-race information from early choices since theoretically early voters have a strong propensity to choose the candidate revealed to them (as we explain in the next section and explore in the experiments). Thus, in the vast majority of the elections we would have revealed to later voters precisely the information that we hypothesize they use horse-race information to infer. Another alternative would have been to assume later voters have no information about the candidates except for the horse-race information, which might be a useful exploration in the future.

Voter Strategies and Equilibria under Simultaneous Voting

We noted above, when voters have complete information about the candidates, then two types of equilibria can occur—either all the voters choose sincerely their most preferred candidates and the election is expected to be a tie between the liberal and conservative candidates or else the liberal or conservative voters choose strategically the moderate candidate, forming an electoral coalition with moderates, and the moderate wins. What happens when voters have incomplete information about the candidates? How then do voters choose in simultaneous voting elections? In sequential voting elections? In this section, we present our theoretical predictions about voter choices when they have incomplete information.

With incomplete information about two of the candidates, a strong bias is induced for the candidate who is known with certainty in simultaneous voting. If that candidate is either the liberal or conservative and her supporters are numerous enough, her supporters have a dominant strategy to vote for her and the other voters have a dominant strategy to randomize between the other two candidates, regardless of the size of α (degree of risk aversion). Given the size of the revealed candidate's supporters, she is likely to win, making voting for her a dominant strategy for her supporters. This result holds only if the supporters are at least a third of the electorate. *Thus, if an extremist (liberal or conservative) candidate is better known than the other candidates and voting is simultaneous, the extremist candidate is likely to win.*

If the "revealed" candidate is the Condorcet winner, the moderate, all voters have a dominant strategy of choosing her if $\alpha > 0.5$ (voters are risk-averse). If $\alpha < 0.5$ (voters are risk-seeking), then only the moderates should choose her, and the other voters should randomize between the unrevealed candidates. *Therefore, if the moderate candidate is better known than the other candidates and voting is simultaneous, the moderate candidate is likely to win if voters are risk-averse.* In summary, then, if either the liberal or conservative candidate is revealed and voting is simultaneous, that candidate will win. If the moderate candidate is revealed, and voters are risk-averse, then the moderate will win. The possible symmetric equilibria under simultaneous voting in our experimental setup are summarized in the following proposition. Proofs of all propositions are presented in appendix B.

PROPOSITION 1: *When voting is simultaneous and voters know the true position of only one of the three candidates, then the following voting equilibria exist:*

1. *If the liberal candidate is known, the liberal candidate is expected to be in first place and the moderate and conservative candidates will be in a close race for second place.*
2. *If the moderate candidate is revealed, the moderate is expected to be in first place and the liberal and conservative candidates are expected to be in a close race for second place if $\alpha > 0.5$, all three candidates are in a close race for first place if $\alpha = 0.5$, and the liberal and conservative candidates are in a close race for first place with the moderate in last place if $\alpha < 0.5$.*
3. *If the conservative candidate is revealed, the conservative candidate is*

*expected to be in first place and the moderate and liberal candidates
will be in a close race for second place.*

Thus, our analysis suggests that when candidates are well known like Dole in
1996, in simultaneous voting, they have a tremendous electoral advantage, regardless of whether the candidate is a moderate or extremist. We now turn to
our analysis of sequential voting elections.

Voter Strategies and Equilibria under Sequential Voting

Information Revelation in Sequential Voting

In the sequential voting elections, early voters know the identity of one of the
candidates and choose. Later voters know the identity of a different candidate
and the outcome of early choices. The first theoretical question to consider in
sequential voting elections is whether early voters should choose "informatively": that is, can the early balloting reveal information to later voters? Specifically, will early choices be such that later voters can, given sufficient information about them, figure out what early voters have been told (given the
information that later voters also know)? We find that the answer to the first part
of the question is yes, early voters should choose "informatively."[5]

In order to give an intuitive understanding of this result, we will work
through some of the possible cases. Consider, for example, the case where early
voters know the policy position of the liberal candidate, later voters know the
policy position of the conservative candidate and α is high (voters are risk-
averse). First, assume that voting is not informative, that early voters use the
same voting strategy regardless of their information. Early voting is thus expected to be random and unrelated to the information they have about the candidates; they will randomly choose across all three candidates—liberal, moderate, and conservative. Later voters then cannot infer what early voters know,
and they only know then the policy position of the conservative candidate.
Later-conservative voters clearly have a weakly dominant or dominant strategy
of always voting for the conservative candidate who is known to them. Later-
liberal and later-moderate voters have a weakly dominant or dominant strategy
of randomizing between the two unknown candidates since their expected utility from randomizing is greater than their expected utility from voting for the
conservative candidate who is known to them.

If early voters' choices are random and unrelated to the information they
know, then the expected outcome of the election will be a win by the conservative candidate. The later-conservative voters will be able to have their most
preferred candidate win. However, in this case early-liberal voters cannot be

maximizing expected utility since their expected utility from voting for the liberal candidate whom they know is greater than any randomization scheme involving voting for one of the other candidates who could then win. Voting randomly would make early-liberal voters worse off in this case than if they voted informatively for the liberal candidate they know. It is straightforward to show that uninformative choices always penalize some early voters by advantaging the candidate known to later voters.

This result is stated formally for all cases in Proposition 2 below.

PROPOSITION 2. *Under sequential voting with incomplete information, early voters will find it expected utility maximizing to choose nonrandomly, or "informatively."*

The lesson to be taken from our analysis is that early voters, like in New Hampshire, should find it disadvantageous to "hide" the information they have by making random choices. Because the election outcome as a whole depends on all voters' choices, early voters should choose informatively.

Equilibrium Voting Strategies for Early Voters

Since it is not rational for early voters to choose uninformatively, then early voters will choose in order to maximize their expected utility given the information attained. In fact, early voters should choose like voters in simultaneous voting elections where voters know the identity of only one of the three candidates. If early voters know either the liberal or conservative candidate, the supporters of that candidate will vote for their first preference, and supporters of the other two candidates will randomize. If the moderate candidate is known, all early voters will choose him if α is high (voters are risk-averse). If α is low (voters are risk-seeking), then only early-moderate voters will choose the moderate, and liberal and conservative voters will randomize between the two unknown candidates, x and z. Proposition 3 below states this result formally:

PROPOSITION 3. *When voting is sequential, early voting is informative, and early voters know the true position of only one of the three candidates, then early voters will use the following pure strategies:*

1. *If the liberal candidate is known to early voters, early-liberal voters will choose her, and early-moderate and early-conservative voters will randomize between the other two candidates.*
2. *If the moderate candidate is known to early voters, early-moderate voters will choose the moderate. Early-liberal and early-conservative vot-*

ers will vote for the moderate if α > 0.5; if α = 0.5, they will random-ize among all three candidates, and if α < 0.5 they will randomize be-tween the two unknown candidates.

3. *If the conservative candidate is known to early voters, early-conservative voters will choose the conservative candidate, and early-liberal and early-moderate voters will randomize between the other two candidates.*

In summary, early voters are like those in simultaneous voting elections—they choose the "evil" they know (or the "good") unless they are risk-seeking and the moderate candidate is revealed. This early voting can be informative to later voters since it does reflect their preferences.

Equilibrium Voting Strategies for Later Voters

When Later Voters Cannot Learn from Early Balloting
Hence, early voters will not choose randomly, but informatively, reflecting their preferences. But how "informative" are these choices? That is, since the early balloting is partly random, will later voters really be able always to infer the information that early voters have? Consider the example above when early voters know the policy position of the liberal candidate and later voters know the policy position of the conservative candidate. Assume also that later voters know the outcome of early choices by voter type. Later voters will therefore know the identity of the conservative candidate and that early voters know something about one of the other two candidates; they will observe that all of the early-liberal voters have chosen one of these two candidates and that early-moderate and early-conservative voters have not (and apparently randomly between the conservative candidate later voters know and the other candidate later voters do not know). Later voters can infer the identity of the liberal candidate since she received all the ballots of the early-liberal voters but none of the early-moderate and early-conservative voters' choices.

When later voters only know the aggregate outcome of early balloting, the inference is also possible, but in some cases the randomization of choices may prevent later voters from distinguishing whether the liberal or moderate candidate is known to early voters. Later voters should also have more difficulty distinguishing early voter information when α is low (voters are risk-seeking), since in that case all early voters should not choose the moderate if they know her policy position. While it is still rational for early voters to choose informatively in these cases (not voting informatively would leave the outcome to the preferences of later voters as above), later voters may not be able, in some circumstances, to infer the information that early voters have. When later voters cannot infer the information that early voters have, later voters will choose as predicted in simultaneous voting given the information that they have been given. This is summarized in Proposition 4:

PROPOSITION 4. *When voting is sequential and later voters are unable to infer the information early voters have (either due to randomization in early balloting or because they do not know the voting by voter type), then later voters will use the following pure strategies:*

1. *If the liberal candidate is known to later voters, later-liberal voters will choose her, and later-moderate and later-conservative voters will randomize between the other two candidates.*
2. *If the moderate candidate is known to later voters, later-moderate voters will choose the moderate. Later-liberal and later-conservative voters will choose the moderate if $\alpha > 0.5$; if $\alpha = 0.5$, they will randomize among all three candidates, and if $\alpha < 0.5$ they will randomize between the two unknown candidates.*
3. *If the conservative candidate is known to later voters, later-conservative voters will choose the conservative candidate, and later-liberal and later-moderate voters will randomize between the other two candidates.*

Later voters, then, who cannot learn from early balloting are just like voters in simultaneous voting elections or early voters in sequential voting elections— they will choose the candidate that is well-known to them in most cases.

When Later Voters Can Learn from Early Balloting
But in some cases, later voters will be able to infer information by observing early choices. What are the predicted strategies for later voters when they are able to infer the identity of all three candidates? Later-moderate voters will always have a weakly dominant or dominant strategy of choosing the moderate candidate, since they prefer him to either the liberal or conservative candidates and are indifferent between the liberal and conservative candidates. However, as noted above, later-liberal and later-conservative voters have a choice between voting strategically for the moderate (forming an electoral coalition with moderates) or sincerely for their first preference. What they will choose will depend on their perceptions of the possible election outcomes, just as in the complete-information simultaneous-voting elections we discussed earlier in this chapter. Moreover, because of the randomization possible in early balloting, our predictions of later voting depend on the outcome of early choices. In some circumstances, only equilibria with strategic voting by later-liberal and later-conservative voters are predicted, and, in others, both strategic and sincere equi-

libria are predicted. In appendix B we go through some examples. We summarize our predictions of the sequential voting equilibria in Proposition 5:

PROPOSITION 5. *When voting is sequential, early voters know the position of only one of the three candidates, and later voters know the position of a different candidate and are able to infer from early outcomes early voters' information, then there are two types of equilibria possible: sincere voting equilibria in which all later voters choose sincerely for their first preferences or strategic voting equilibria in which either later-liberal and/or later-conservative voters choose the moderate candidate. These equilibria and the electoral outcomes depend upon the potential randomization of early balloting. When the moderate candidate is revealed to early voters and $\alpha > 0.5$, then in all the equilibria the moderate candidate is the expected winner. When the liberal or conservative candidate is revealed to early voters or the moderate is revealed and $\alpha \leq 0.5$ then multiple equilibria typically exist in which the expected winner varies.*

Therefore, which candidate wins, when later voters are able to learn, depends on the distribution of knowledge about the candidates across early and later voters and the degree of voter risk aversion, as well as random factors. In general, because of the randomness, it is possible that any of the three candidates can win. If the moderate candidate is revealed to early voters and voters are risk-averse, then the moderate candidate can use success in early balloting to build momentum-like electoral success.

Summary of the Equilibrium Predictions

Our theoretical analysis thus yields a number of important predictions:

1. When voting is simultaneous as in a national primary or other elections held at the same time, the better-known candidate is most likely to win if extremist. If the better-known candidate is a moderate, she is likely to win when voters are risk-averse.
2. When voting is sequential, early voters should choose informatively (that is, later voters may be able to infer from their balloting the information that earlier voters have).
3. When voting is sequential as in drawn-out primaries or in mail-in and early balloting, both extremists and moderates can win depending on whether extremist voters choose strategically their second preferences or sincerely their first. Their tendencies to do so will depend on their expectations of what other voters will do as well as their degree of risk aversion.

In the next two chapters, we present our experimental design and analysis. We examine whether the voting behavior and outcomes of the elections differ with the voting systems in chapter 6. In chapter 7, we consider the effect of representativeness of early voters on voting behavior and election outcomes. Through our experiments we investigate these questions: Do voters choose as predicted? Are candidates elected under the different systems different? Do later voters learn? Does representativeness of early voters matter?

CHAPTER 6

Simultaneous versus Sequential Voting

Our theoretical study of simultaneous and sequential voting is just the first step in our analysis. Now we consider an empirical evaluation of the theory. First, we need to operationalize our model's assumptions in an experimental design. We need to create a laboratory world that can evaluate our election story. In this chapter we discuss our design (our laboratory world) and then present the results of our experimental analysis of simultaneous versus sequential voting elections.[1]

Our Laboratory Election Environment

While in our discussion of the theoretical model we call the candidates *liberal, moderate,* and *conservative* and the voters *liberals, moderates,* or *conservatives,* in the experiments we did not use these labels because of the values that voters may place on them. Instead, we called the liberal candidate *x,* the moderate candidate *y,* and the conservative candidate *z.* We called liberal voters *type 1,* moderate voters *type 2,* and conservative voters *type 3.* In total, there were ten liberal voters, four moderate voters, and ten conservative voters in each election.

In the laboratory elections, we used two payoff configurations. We used two different configurations to measure the effects of risk aversion of liberal and conservative voters on ballot choices and electoral outcomes. In the risk-averse manipulation $\alpha = 0.8$ and in the risk-seeking manipulation $\alpha = 0.25$. Table 6.1 presents the payoffs used in the experiments (note that to solve for α we normalize the payoff a subject received from the candidate she preferred least at 0 and the payoff she received from her first preference at 1). On average subjects in the experiments earned about $22.00 each.

One problem we face in our experimental design is that our subjects may be risk-averse in monetary payoffs, and this may mean that our risk-seeking manipulation does not have the desired effect. That is, if the subjects are risk-averse in the money they receive from participating in the experiment, the true value of α for them is greater than either 0.8 or 0.25. If the true value is greater than 0.5 in the risk-seeking treatment, then liberals and conservatives in the risk-seeking treatment should make the same choices that they would make in the risk-averse treatment.

TABLE 6.1.   Voter Payoff Matrix in Experiments

Voter Types	x (Liberal)	y (Moderate)	z (Conservative)	Number of Voters
Low α Treatment (Risk-Seeking Manipulation)				
1 (liberals)	$1.30	$0.55	$0.30	10
2 (moderates)	$0.55	$1.30	$0.55	4
3 (conservatives)	$0.30	$0.55	$1.30	10
High α Treatment (Risk-Averse Manipulation)				
1 (liberals)	$1.10	$0.90	$0.15	10
2 (moderates)	$0.90	$1.10	$0.90	4
3 (conservatives)	$0.10	$0.90	$1.10	10

Voters were randomly reassigned types before each election. The types were also randomly reordered before each election. We used these measures to reduce repeated-game effects. If voters are the same types for a series of elections, they may be making choices that are optimal for the series of elections rather than the single election we are analyzing. While voter behavior in repeated elections is important and worthy of future study, this was not our focus in these experiments. Moreover, while elections in a given state may seem at first glance to be best viewed as repeated contests with the same electorates and party choices, there are random changes that occur making each election distinct (changes in the electorate and candidates over time). Thus, we believe that a one-shot game captures what elections are like in this context.

Voters were given full information about the distribution of voter types. However, voters did not know the specific identities of the other voters. For example, voters knew that there were 10 voters of type 1 but did not know which of the other subjects were of type 1. Voter perceptions in the naturally occurring environment can be affected by an assortment of uncertainties about the demographics of voters, positions of the candidates, voter preferences over the candidates, turnout, and how voters will choose given their information. In our experiments, we remove some of the uncertainty. We give all voters information on the number of types of voters and how each type ranks the candidates by monetary payoffs. Yet, voters do not know how the other voters value these payoffs, the uncertainty that they have on how other voters value the payoffs, and how the other voters will choose based on their payoffs. This preference and strategic uncertainty can lead to much doubt in voters' minds about the electoral outcome even though they may know the numbers of types of voters and the payoffs by types.

We conducted 250 laboratory elections at Michigan State University, drawing from a subject pool recruited from the population of students attending undergraduate classes. In each laboratory election, we used 24 subjects. We conducted 10 sessions of 25 elections each with a total of 240 subjects and 6,000 individual voting decisions.

When the subjects arrived they were seated and given copies of the instructions for the session. Instructions for sequential voting are contained in appendix C. The instructions were read aloud and questions were answered in public. While the instructions carefully explain the nature of the experiment, they do not suggest to the subjects how they should vote or strategies they should use. We gave the subjects a short true/false quiz on the instructions, and then in public we addressed areas of the instructions that the quiz demonstrated the subjects did not understand. In general, the results of the quiz do show that the subjects understood the instructions. A copy of the quiz is also included in appendix C.

The experiment was conducted over a computer network. A computer program was used to allocate types, assign payoffs, record payoffs, and provide records of total earnings and all transactions. After the quiz, the subjects were seated at computer terminals in a large classroom. While dividers did not separate the subjects, the display of the computer program was designed such that the screen could not be read from more than three feet away. The sessions each lasted about 2 hours total, with approximately 45 minutes to one hour of instruction. In a posttreatment survey 96 percent of the subjects reported that they felt they understood the rules of the experiment and 99 percent reported that they were happy with their payoffs. It is important to note that our experiments are not simulations of the election processes, but real elections in which the subjects made real choices that affected their payments.

Operationalizing Information Asymmetries

In order to capture the potential effects of incomplete information in the experiment, candidates were labeled Green, Orange, or Blue in the laboratory elections. Before each election, the candidates were randomly assigned as either *x, y,* or *z* such that there was a one-to-one correspondence between candidate labels and types. Voters initially were not told this correspondence. Voters knew then the distribution of candidate types but not the identity of particular candidates. Before each election, voters were told the truthful identity of one of the candidates as described below.

TABLE 6.2. **Summary of Experimental Design: Simultaneous and Sequential Voting**

	Simultaneous Voting Treatments	Sequential Voting Treatments	Totals
High α (risk-averse voters)	25 elections with 24 subjects each = 600 voting decisions	100 elections with 24 subjects each = 2,400 voting decisions	125 elections with 24 subjects each = 3,000 voting decisions
Low α (risk-seeking voters)	25 elections with 24 subjects each = 600 voting decisions	100 elections with 24 subjects each = 2,400 voting decisions	125 elections with 24 subjects each = 3,000 voting decisions
Totals	50 elections with 24 subjects each = 1,200 voting decisions	200 elections with 24 subjects each = 4,800 voting decisions	250 elections with 24 subjects each = 6,000 voting decisions

We considered two types of voting processes under our incomplete information setup: simultaneous (like in the virtual national primary or elections held on a single day) and sequential voting (like in drawn-out primaries or in mail-in and early balloting). We conducted ten sessions in the experiment, two using simultaneous voting (one with high α—risk-averse manipulation and the other with low α—risk-seeking manipulation) and eight using sequential voting (four with high α—risk-averse manipulation—and four with low α—risk-seeking manipulation). Thus, we conducted 50 simultaneous voting elections and 200 sequential voting elections. Table 6.2 presents an overview of our experimental design.

Simultaneous Voting Elections

Recall that we assume that in simultaneous voting elections all voters know the policy position of one candidate but not the positions of the other two. In our experiments, we operationalized this in the simultaneous treatments by truthfully revealing to all voters one of the candidates, Green, Orange, or Blue, as either x, y, or z. For example, voters might have been told that Orange was actually x. Voters would know that either Blue was y and Green was z or vice versa. After one of the candidates was revealed, then all voters chose, and payoffs were allocated to voters according to whether candidate x, y, or z won. If the election was a tie, the winner was randomly selected between the tied candidates. As noted in chapter 5, our simultaneous voting elections are designed to capture the case of the virtual national primary where voters know well one particular candidate, like Dole in 1996, or in single-day elections.

Sequential Voting Elections

In the sequential voting treatments, before an election each voter was randomly assigned to an initial voting group, A (early voters) or B (later voters). Each voting group had 12 of the 24 subjects. We conducted two types of distributions of the subjects across voting groups. In the *representative early voter* treatment (Sequential 1), each group had 5 liberal voters, 2 moderates, and 5 conservatives. In the *nonrepresentative early voter* treatment (Sequential 2), group A (early voters) was comprised of 10 liberals and 2 moderates and group B (later voters) was comprised of 10 conservatives and 2 moderates. We discuss the effects of representativeness in chapter 7.

In the sequential voting elections, first one of the candidates is randomly revealed as either *x*, *y*, or *z* to voters in group A (early voters). Next, voters in group A choose. Group A's choices are then revealed to all the subjects. We revealed this information in two ways, as discussed in chapter 5. In the *low-information* treatment we simply informed group B (later voters) the aggregate outcome of group A voting, that is, the number of votes received by Orange, Blue, and Green. The low-information treatment is probably more likely to capture the case of sequential voting in early and mail-in balloting. We conducted four low-information sequential-voting treatments for 100 low-information sequential-voting elections. In the *high-information* treatment group B (later) voters were told how group A (early) voters chose by voter type. That is, later voters were told how type 1 voters voted, how type 2 voters chose, and so on. We also conducted four high-information sequential-voting treatments for 100 high-information sequential-voting elections.

After group B was informed of the choices of group A, a different candidate was revealed to group B, and group B chose. Payoffs were allocated to voters according to whether candidate *x*, *y*, or *z* won with the same tie-breaking procedure if necessary. Figure 6.1 presents a diagram of how the sequential voting process worked, and table 6.3 summarizes how the sequential voting treatments were distributed across high and low information and risk-averse and risk-seeking treatments.

Experimental Results in Simultaneous Voting Elections

Our theoretical analysis predicts that candidates revealed are more likely to win in simultaneous voting in the high α treatment (risk-averse voters) and when either the liberal or conservative candidate is revealed in the low α treatment (risk-seeking voters). We can state these predictions more formally as the following hypotheses:

**Group A (early voters) are told
the identity of one of the candidates**

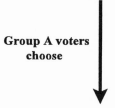

**Group A voters
choose**

**Group B (later voters) are told
the identity of one of the other candidates
and the outcome of Group A voting**

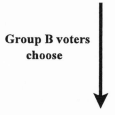

**Group B voters
choose**

**Votes Added
Winner Declared**

**Subjects randomly reassigned
types and groups**

Fig. 6.1.   Election process in sequential voting experiments

HYPOTHESIS 1. *In the high α simultaneous voting treatment (risk-averse voters), candidates revealed are more likely to win than other candidates.*

HYPOTHESIS 2. *In the low α simultaneous voting treatment (risk-seeking voters), when either the liberal or conservative candidate is revealed, that candidate is more likely to win than other candidates, but the moderate candidate, if revealed, is less likely to win than other candidates.*

We test these against the following null hypothesis:

HYPOTHESIS 0_a: *Candidates revealed are no more likely to win than other candidates in simultaneous voting regardless of the size of α.*

TABLE 6.3. Summary of Sequential Voting Treatments by Information and Risk Aversion

	Sequential Voting Treatments		
	High Information (Early Outcomes Told to Later Voters by Early Voter Type)	Low Information (Early Outcomes Told to Later Voters in Aggregate Only)	Totals
High α (risk-averse voters)	50 elections with 24 subjects each = 1,200 voting decisions	50 elections with 24 subjects each = 1,200 voting decisions	100 elections with 24 subjects each = 2,400 voting decisions
Low α (risk-seeking voters)	50 elections with 24 subjects each = 1,200 voting decisions	50 elections with 24 subjects each = 1,200 voting decisions	100 elections with 24 subjects each = 2,400 voting decisions
Totals	100 elections with 24 subjects each = 2,400 voting decisions	100 elections with 24 subjects each = 2,400 voting decisions	200 elections with 24 subjects each = 4,800 voting decisions

Figure 6.2 presents the data on candidate wins in the two simultaneous treatments. In the high α treatment (risk-averse voters) we find that the candidate revealed never loses outright (24 wins and 1 two-way tie), which is statistically greater than chance. In the low α treatment (risk-seeking voters) the probability that the candidate revealed wins is also significantly greater than chance but significantly less than in the high α treatment (16 wins, 5 two-way ties, and 4 losses). Although generally supportive of our predictions, the distribution of losses and two-way ties in the low α treatment (3 for the liberal and conservative candidates) is surprising since our prediction is that the moderate candidate is less likely to win when revealed in the low α treatment, not the liberal and conservative candidates.

Since the number of elections we examine is not large, these differences may merely reflect voter errors committed in early periods idiosyncratic to one of the treatments. Our predictions about candidate wins depend on voters using the predicted equilibrium strategies. We therefore consider the following hypotheses about voter strategies in simultaneous voting elections:

HYPOTHESIS 3. *When either the liberal or conservative candidate is revealed, the voters who most prefer that candidate will choose that candidate (liberals and conservatives, respectively) and the other voters will randomize between the other two unrevealed candidates.*

HYPOTHESIS 4. *When the moderate candidate is revealed, all voters will choose him in the high α treatment (risk-averse manipulation). In the low α treatment (risk-seeking manipulation) only moderate voters will choose him.*

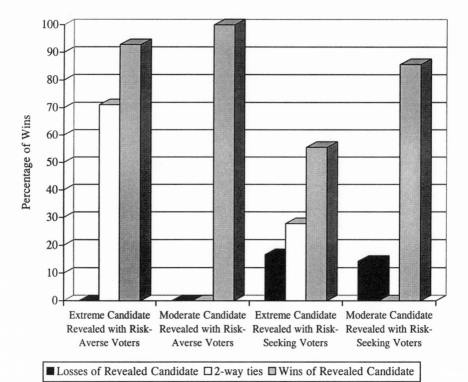

Fig. 6.2. Percentage of wins by revealed candidate in simultaneous voting elections

We test these hypotheses against the following null hypothesis:

HYPOTHESIS 0_b. *Voter choices are unaffected by the candidate revealed or the size of α (degree of risk aversion).*

Figures 6.3 and 6.4 summarize data on the choices made by voters in the simultaneous voting elections. In 90 percent of the 1,200 voting decisions in the two simultaneous treatments the subjects chose as predicted, which is substantially greater than chance. One tendency that subjects may have is always to choose the candidate revealed, regardless of the expected payoff. Assuming that voters always choose the revealed candidate explains only 57.46 percent of the decisions. Yet, if we restrict our analysis to the 10 percent of unpredicted votes, 82.35 percent are votes for the revealed candidate when the prediction is that the voter chooses an unrevealed candidate. Thus, unpredicted votes appear

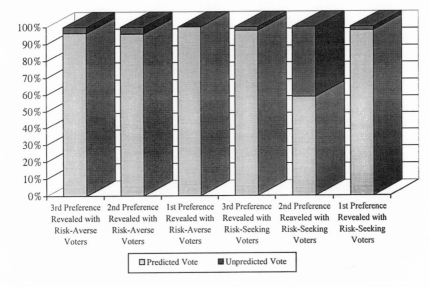

Fig. 6.3. Liberal and conservative voters' choices in simultaneous voting elections

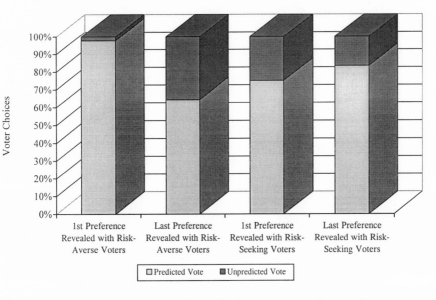

Fig. 6.4. Moderate voters' choices in simultaneous voting elections

to reflect a tendency to choose a revealed candidate. It is useful to examine whether the deviations from the predicted strategies varied with voter type and/or the size of α (degree of risk aversion). Therefore, below we consider the behavior of the different types of voters in the simultaneous voting treatment as compared to the specific predictions.

Liberal and Conservative Voter Decisions in Simultaneous Elections

As predicted, when liberal and conservative voters are told the identity of their least preferred candidate, they choose an unrevealed candidate approximately 96 percent of the time in the high α treatment (risk-averse treatment) and 98 percent of the time in the low α treatment (risk-seeking treatment). When they are told the identity of their first preference, they choose as predicted their first preference 100 percent of the time in the high α treatment and 98 percent of the time in the low α treatment. When their second preference is revealed, the moderate candidate, they choose as predicted (voting for the moderate) 96 percent of the time in the high α treatment but they choose as predicted (voting for either the liberal or conservative candidates) only 59 percent of the time in the low α treatment.

As predicted, the reduction in α (reduction in risk aversion) significantly reduces the number of liberal and conservative voters who choose the moderate candidate, yet there is still a significant percentage of voters who continue to choose him. This is a sign that some of the subjects are risk-averse in the monetary payoffs, since our predictions depend on an assumption of risk neutrality in monetary payoffs. As discussed earlier, risk aversion in monetary payoffs implies a higher true value of α and a greater willingness to choose the moderate rather than the lottery between the liberal and conservative candidates.

Moderate Voter Decisions in Simultaneous Elections

In general, moderate voters also choose significantly as predicted. However, there are more deviations from the predicted strategies among moderate voters than there are among the liberals and conservatives. In the high α treatment (risk-averse voters), moderates display a tendency to choose the revealed candidate when this is unpredicted (doing so in 20 out of 56 cases, i.e., 35.71 percent of the time), and in the low α treatment (risk-seeking voters), moderates display a tendency to choose an unrevealed candidate when this is unpredicted (7 out of 28 cases, i.e., 25 percent of the time). A reduction in unpredicted choices accompanies the decrease in α, which effectively is a decrease in the payoff to moderates from their least preferred alternatives and an increase in the cost of voting for the revealed candidate when this is unpredicted. Recall that for moderate voters α is not a measure of risk aversion, but the payoff a moderate voter receives when one of her least preferred candidates are elected. The cost to moderates of either the liberal or conservative candidates being elected is greater when α is decreased.

In conclusion, we find that voters in the simultaneous voting elections choose overall as expected (90 percent of the decisions). The vast majority of the 10 percent of unpredicted choices, 82.35 percent, are votes for a revealed candidate. As predicted, decreasing α (decreasing risk aversion) does affect voter decisions significantly: liberals and conservatives choose the moderate candidate less when α declines. However, some liberals and conservatives (41.43 percent) appear risk-averse in monetary payoffs and continue to choose the moderate when he is revealed and α is low. Moderate voters' errors are also affected by the size of α: when α is high they tend to choose revealed candidates even when these candidates are not their first choice, and when α is low (and these mistakes are potentially more costly to them) they make fewer errors. We now turn to our analysis of sequential voting under asymmetric information as in drawn-out primaries or early and mail-in balloting.

Experimental Analysis of Sequential Voting under Incomplete Information

In chapter 1, we noted that there are two principal concerns about the virtual national primary and single-day elections (simultaneous voting) and drawn-out primaries and mail-in and early balloting (sequential voting): whether sequential voting allows voters to make more informed choices and whether the representativeness of early voters affects the electoral outcome in sequential voting. We consider in this section how the asymmetric distribution of information affects voter decisions and electoral outcomes in sequential voting. We will discuss the representation issue in the next chapter.

Election Winners in Sequential versus Simultaneous Voting

The argument that sequential voting allows voters to make more informed choices than in simultaneous voting has two parts: (1) candidates elected under simultaneous and sequential voting are different and (2) later voters in sequential voting gain information through the voting process about the distribution of candidates. We will first consider how candidates elected under the two systems vary.

In simultaneous voting elections, the assumption is that voters are all exposed to candidates during the same campaign and one candidate is better known to all voters. This candidate is expected to win. We found in the simultaneous voting elections that the revealed candidate was significantly likely to win, but less so as α (risk aversion) was reduced. In sequential voting elections, in contrast, the campaign provides different pieces of information about the candidates to the voters, and later voters also know how the earlier ones chose. Thus, theoretically the candidate revealed first or better known to the first voters is not as likely to win as she would be if she were the revealed candidate in the simultaneous treatments when that candidate is the liberal or conservative candidate when α is high and in general when α is low.

Our analysis above suggests that the ability of the candidate revealed to early voters to win is related to candidate type. As the Condorcet winner, the moderate candidate would defeat either the liberal or conservative candidate in a pairwise competition, although his supporters are a minority of the electorate. Thus, if either the liberal or conservative candidate is elected, then the voters have chosen a candidate that is preferred less than one of the losers. It is useful then to compare whether the type of voting (simultaneous vs. sequential) leads to more or fewer wins by the moderate candidate.

Furthermore, the comparison above assumes that the candidate revealed first is the same candidate that would be revealed to the voters in the simultaneous voting. The assumption is that front-runners who are better known nationally in the virtual national primary are also the candidates who are better known to early voters in sequential drawn-out primaries or that candidates that are best known in single-day elections are the same as candidates well-known by early voters in mail-in and early balloting. This may not be the case. Therefore, it is useful to compare the electoral success by the type of candidate. The hypotheses below summarize our theoretical predictions:

HYPOTHESIS 5. *Candidates revealed first have a lower chance of winning in sequential voting elections than candidates revealed in simultaneous voting elections.*

HYPOTHESIS 6. *The moderate candidate is more likely to win in sequential than in simultaneous voting elections.*

We test these hypotheses against the following null hypothesis:

HYPOTHESIS 0_c. *Candidates elected under simultaneous and sequential voting elections do not differ.*

Figure 6.5 presents data on the eventual electoral success of candidates revealed to early voters in the sequential voting elections and provides our evaluation of Hypothesis 5. The candidate revealed to early voters won significantly

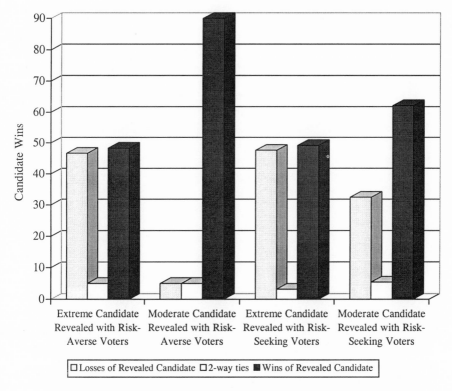

Fig. 6.5. **Percentage of wins by candidate revealed to early voters in simultaneous voting elections**

more than by chance, 119 of 200 elections or 59.5 percent of the time, and tied for first in 9 elections or 4.5 percent of the time. But compared to the revealed candidate in the simultaneous voting elections (who won 40 out of the 50 elections, 80 percent of the time, and tied for first in 6 elections, 12 percent of the time), the candidate revealed to early voters is in general significantly less likely to win.[2]

A simple comparison of electoral success of the moderate candidate in the two election systems shows that while the moderate does win a greater percentage of sequential voting elections (94 wins out of 200 elections, 47 percent, with 11 ties for first place, 5.5 percent) than simultaneous elections (19 wins out of 50 elections, 38 percent, with 3 ties for first place, 6 percent) the difference is insignificant.[3] Overall, the moderate wins less often when revealed to early voters in the sequential elections than when revealed to all voters in the simultaneous elections.[4]

But the ability of the moderate candidate to win should depend on the size of α (risk aversion); when α is high the moderate candidate is the expected winner in both simultaneous and sequential voting, but not when α is low. In the sequential high α treatments, the moderate candidate was revealed to early voters in 40 out of 100 of the elections, winning 36 and tying for first place twice. We cannot compare this statistically to the simultaneous voting elections when α is high since the moderate won in 100 percent of the elections in which he was revealed to all voters. In the sequential low α treatments, the moderate was revealed to early voters in 37 elections, winning 28 and tying for first place twice. As expected, there is a significant difference in the success rate of the moderate candidate between the high and low α treatments in the sequential voting elections.[5] However, the success rate of the moderate in the low α is not significantly different from the percentage of wins when the moderate is revealed to voters in the simultaneous voting elections.[6] Thus, the evidence suggests that when the moderate candidate is revealed to early voters, the electoral outcome is significantly different from when he is revealed to all voters in simultaneous voting elections when α is high but less so when α is low.

These results seem to suggest that simultaneous voting may advantage the moderate candidate more than sequential voting. But the moderate candidate also wins a number of elections in sequential voting when he is not revealed to early voters (i.e., is not the first revealed candidate), 35 out of 123 elections (28.46 percent), tying for first place in 5.69 percent of the elections. This is significantly more than the success rate of the moderate candidate when the liberal or conservative candidates were revealed in the simultaneous voting elections.[7] When either the liberal or conservative candidate is revealed to early voters that candidate wins 48.33 percent of the time (29/60) when α is high (with 3/60 ties for first place) and 49.21 percent of the time (31/63) when α is low (with 2/63 first place ties). There is no statistical difference between these two success rates in sequential voting elections by the value of α, as predicted.[8] However, the candidate revealed to early voters, when either liberal or conservative, is statistically less likely to win than when either the liberal or conservative candidate is revealed to voters in simultaneous elections.[9] Thus, the liberal and conservative candidates win significantly less often when revealed to early voters in the sequential voting elections than when revealed to all voters in the simultaneous voting elections.

These combined results suggest that the moderate candidate may be more likely to win in sequential voting than in simultaneous voting. While instructive, with the simple analysis it is difficult to control for the combined effects of other variables on the likelihood that the moderate wins, variables such as the size of α, whether later voters had low or high information about early voters' choices, the election period (if "learning" by the subjects takes place during the experiment this may either increase or decrease the likelihood of the moderate candidate winning), and whether the moderate candidate is revealed to later voters. In order to determine the combined effects of these variables, we estimated a multivariate equation of the probability that the moderate candidate wins as a function of these variables as well as whether the voting was simultaneous or sequential. Since our dependent variable was the probability that the moderate candidate wins, we used logit analysis (see Aldrich and Nelson 1984 for a discussion of logit). The results of this estimation are reported in table D1 in appendix D.[10]

We summarize the predictions that result from our estimation in table 6.4, which presents the predicted probabilities of the moderate candidate winning under different possible situations. First, notice that when the moderate candidate is not revealed, either to simultaneous voters or to either group of sequential voters, the moderate candidate is much more likely to win in the sequential voting elections regardless of the detail of the information provided to later voters and the size of α (degree of risk aversion). With α is high (voters are risk-averse), the moderate candidate is predicted to win only 29 percent of the time when not revealed in simultaneous voting elections. But in the sequential voting elections, she is predicted to win 60 percent of the time when later voters have detailed information on early choices and 40 percent of the time when later voters only have aggregate information on early balloting. Similarly, when α is low (voters are risk-seeking), the moderate candidate is predicted to win when not revealed in simultaneous voting elections only 18 percent of the time. But in the sequential voting elections, she is predicted to win 46 percent of the time

TABLE 6.4. Predicted Moderate Candidate's Probability of Winning (in percentages)

			Sequential Voting					
	Simultaneous Voting		Moderate Not Revealed		Moderate Revealed to Early Voters		Moderate Revealed to Later Voters	
	Liberal or Conservative Candidate Revealed	Moderate Candidate Revealed	High Information	Low Information	High Information	Low Information	High Information	Low Information
High α (risk-averse voters)	29	97	60	40	94	87	65	44
Low α (risk-seeking voters)	18	95	46	26	90	79	50	30

Note: Period = 25 and calculated using values in table D1.

when later voters have detailed information on early choices and 26 percent of the time when later voters only have aggregate information on early balloting. *When the moderate candidate is unlikely to be known, she is much more likely to win in sequential voting elections than in simultaneous voting elections.*

However, when the moderate candidate is revealed to simultaneous voters, she is more likely to win in these elections than in the sequential elections even when she is revealed to early voters, later voters have detailed information on earlier choices, and voters are risk-averse (97 to 94 percent predicted probability). When voters are risk-seeking the comparison is between 95 and 90 percent. When the moderate candidate is revealed to later voters or not revealed, simultaneous voting elections are hugely more likely to result in wins for the moderate. *When moderates are known to simultaneous voters, they are more likely to be elected in simultaneous than in sequential voting elections. Our results then suggest that when a front-runner is a moderate the virtual national primary or single-day election (simultaneous voting) is more likely to lead to moderate wins than drawn-out primaries or mail-in and early balloting (sequential voting). When the front-runner is an extremist, the virtual national primary or single-day elections lead to fewer moderate wins than in drawn-out primaries or mail-in and early balloting. Thus, the type of candidate elected is likely to be different across voting systems depending on which candidate is the front-runner.*

Do Early Voters Choose Informatively?

The second proposed advantage of drawn-out primaries (sequential voting) over the virtual national primary (simultaneous voting) is the supposition that later voters become more informed than they otherwise would by observing the choices of earlier voters. This is also a potential advantage in mail-in and early balloting if news reports on early choices are available. For this to occur the early voters would need to choose informatively, choosing as voters in the simultaneous voting treatment, as discussed above.[11] We state this prediction in the following hypothesis, Hypothesis 7, which we evaluate versus the null hypothesis, Hypothesis 0_d:

HYPOTHESIS 7. *Early voters choose informatively, that is, reflecting the information they are told about the candidates, and as voters in the simultaneous voting elections choose.*

HYPOTHESIS 0_d. *Early voters vote randomly.*

Figures 6.6 and 6.7 summarize the decisions of early voters in the sequential voting elections. Of the 2,400 decisions of early voters, 87.08 percent

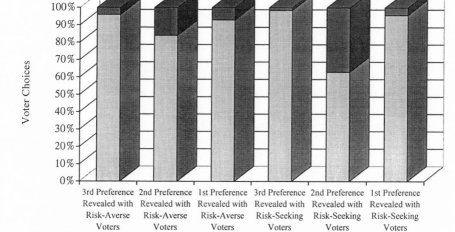

Fig. 6.6. Liberal and conservative early voters' choices in sequential voting elections

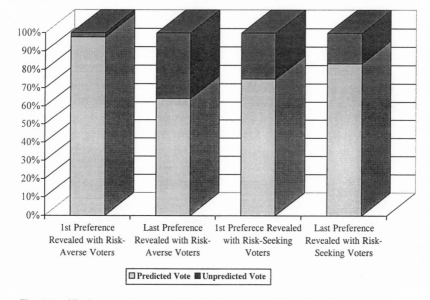

Fig. 6.7. Moderate early voters' choices in sequential voting elections

are as predicted for informative voting. This percentage is large, but it is significantly less than the percentage of predicted choices in the simultaneous voting elections.[12] As in the simultaneous voting elections, early voters have a tendency to choose the candidate revealed, 53.88 percent of the time. Of the unpredicted choices in the sequential voting elections, 66.77 percent were for the revealed candidate, which is less than in the simultaneous voting elections.

As in the simultaneous voting elections, early voters generally choose their first preference if revealed. As α decreases (voters are risk-seeking), early-liberal and early-conservative voters choose the moderate candidate less when he is revealed (84 percent decreases to 62.97 percent). Early-moderate voters, as in the simultaneous elections, have a tendency to choose revealed candidates even when unpredicted in the high α treatment (risk-averse voters), but less so in the low α treatment (risk-seeking voters).

Do Later Voters Learn?

These results support the contention that early voters choose informatively. However, do later voters use the results from early choices in their decisions and, if so, how? Do they learn from the choices of the early voters? As discussed in chapter 5, if later voters do not use the results from early voting as an information source they should choose as voters in the simultaneous voting elections with respect to the candidate revealed to them. We state this prediction as Hypothesis 8, which we test against the null Hypothesis 0_e:

HYPOTHESIS 8. *Later voters' decisions are influenced by the outcome of early choices.*

HYPOTHESIS 0_e. *Later voters' decisions are unaffected by the outcome of early choices.*

A first glance suggests that later voters' decisions may not be influenced by early choices. Of the 2,400 voting decisions, 81.25 percent are consistent with the predicted voting decisions assuming the later voters do not use the results of early choices. That is, if later voters do not use early balloting results, they should choose as in simultaneous voting elections. Figures 6.8 and 6.9 present detailed data on later balloting decisions with respect to the candidate revealed to later voters as compared to the predicted choices if they ignored early voters' choices.

But it would be premature to conclude from this analysis that later voters do not use early choices to infer information about the candidates. Many of these ballots are also consistent with equilibria in which later voters choose with complete information, using the outcome of early choices. Specifically, later-

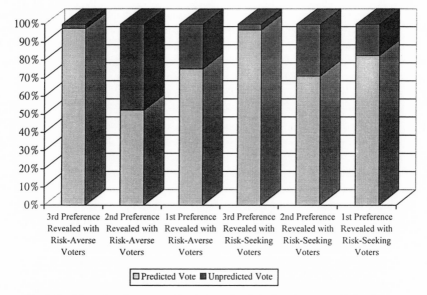

Fig. 6.8. Liberal and conservative later voters' choices in sequential voting elections ignoring early voting outcomes

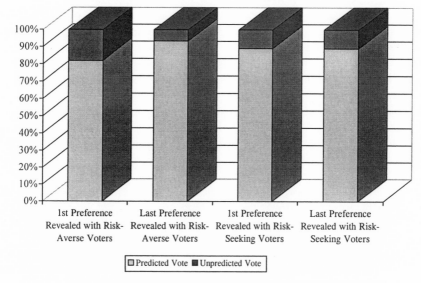

Fig. 6.9. Moderate later voters' choices in sequential voting elections ignoring early voting outcomes

moderate voters' ballots under complete information will be consistent with their choices assuming they do not use the results of early voting. And later-liberal and later-conservative voters should, under complete information, never choose for their third preference, which is consistent with the prediction, that these voters ignored early choices and their third preference is revealed. Finally, as shown in Proposition 5 in chapter 5, equilibria exist in which later-liberal and later-conservative voters may choose sincerely their first preference or strategically their second, and in all but one of the elections both of these equilibria are possible, depending on the outcome of early choices.[13] Hence, distinguishing when later voter behavior is influenced by early balloting is difficult.

Evidence that later voters may be using the information from early balloting exists if later voters choose unpredictably their second or first preference. That is, if later voters choose significantly their first preference when their second preference is revealed to them or if later voters choose significantly their second preference when their first preference is revealed to them, then later voters may be using the results of early balloting in making their choices since otherwise they should choose randomly. Examination of the choices of later-liberal and later-conservative voters does suggest that these voters may be so influenced. When their first preference is revealed to them, they do not choose that candidate 24.78 percent of the time, which is significantly greater than the percentage observed of early-liberal and early-conservative voters (7.04 percent) or liberal and conservative voters in the simultaneous voting elections (0 percent). Of these "unpredicted" votes, 80.72 percent (67/83) are for the moderate candidate, suggesting that these voters use the outcome of early balloting to infer the moderate's identity and chose to vote for him instead of their first preference even though their first preference was revealed to them.

In the high α treatment (risk-averse voters) there are also a significant percentage of later-liberal and later-conservative voters not choosing their second preference when revealed to them, 47.58 percent of the time, which is greater than 16 percent of the same types of voters in the early voting group and 4.09 percent of the same voters in the simultaneous voting elections. Of these choices, 75.80 percent (119/157) are for the voters' first preference instead, which suggests that the voters are using the results of early balloting to infer the identity of their first preference. However, when α is low (risk-seeking voters), these later voters choose more often their second preference when revealed to them as compared to the same types of early voters and those in the simultaneous voting elections. Moreover, all of the unpredicted choices in this case are actually for the voters' third preferences, suggesting that in the low α treatment these voters were not able to use the results of early balloting effectively. The data suggest that in the high α treatment later voters do to some extent use early choices to infer the identity of particular candidates, but less so when α is low.

A more precise way to determine whether later voting is influenced by early choices is to examine the extent that later voters choose their least preferred candidate (suggesting that they do not know the identity of all the candidates) as compared with early voters and voters in the simultaneous voting elections. If later voters gain information through the sequential voting process, there should be significantly fewer of these choices for a voter's least preferred candidate in later balloting than in the simultaneous voting elections and in early balloting in the sequential voting elections. But there are many factors that can affect voters' tendencies to choose their least preferred candidates. There may be some learning during the experiment, and choices in later periods may reflect that. We have seen that as election periods increase, the moderate candidate is more likely to win. As α is decreased (risk-seeking voting), early balloting is more random and harder to determine. Later voters' abilities to infer information from early choices may be affected by the candidate revealed to them and their own types. That is, if an early voter's least preferred candidate is revealed to a later voter then that voter is less likely to choose that candidate regardless of information available from early ballots. Thus, an analysis of the later voter's choices of their least preferred candidates should control for these factors.

In order to determine whether these factors influenced the extent that voters chose their least preferred candidate we report a logit explaining the decision to vote for a voter's least preferred candidate by voter type in table D2 in appendix D.[14] We combine the data for all voters in all treatments in the estimation. The dependent variable in these logits is coded 1 if a voter chose her least preferred candidate (a vote for the liberal candidate for a conservative, a vote for the liberal or conservative candidates for a moderate, and a vote for the conservative candidate for a liberal) and 0 otherwise. Table 6.5 summarizes the implications of the empirical estimation for the predicted probability that a voter will choose her least preferred candidate as a function of various treatment conditions.

Significantly, later voters with detailed information about early balloting do choose their least preferred candidate less than simultaneous or early sequential voters regardless of the degree of risk aversion, voter type, or type of candidate revealed to voter. The biggest effect is observed when moderate voters are not told the identity of the liberal or conservative candidate—moderate simultaneous and early sequential voters are predicted to vote for their least preferred candidate 36 percent of the time when the moderate is not revealed to them, while later-moderate sequential voters are predicted to vote for their least preferred candidate 27 percent of the time when the moderate is not revealed to them and they have detailed information about early choices. However, when later voters do not have detailed information on early voter choices, they make more errors, not fewer. Later-moderate sequential voters are predicted to vote

TABLE 6.5. Predicted Probability Voter Chooses Least Preferred Candidate (in percentages)

		Voter in Simultaneous Voting Election or Early Voter in Sequential Voting		Later Voter in Sequential Voting			
		Liberal or Conservative Candidate Revealed to Voter	Moderate Candidate Revealed to Voter	Liberal or Conservative Candidate Revealed to Voter		Moderate Candidate Revealed to Voter	
				High Information	Low Information	High Information	Low Information
High α (risk-averse voter)	Moderate voter	36	5	27	43	4	7
	Liberal or conservative voter	1	10	1	2	7	13
Low α (risk-seeking voter)	Moderate voter	51	10	42	59	7	13
	Liberal or conservative voter	3	18	2	4	13	22

Note: Period = 25, calculated using values in table D2.

for their least preferred candidate 43 percent of the time when the moderate is not revealed to them and they only have aggregate information on early voting outcomes. *Later voters are predicted to learn by the voting of early voters only when they have detailed information on early voter choices. When information is not detailed, later voters appear to become less informed than they should be!*

The other factors in the analysis have generally predictable effects. Voters are less likely to choose their least preferred candidate when the moderate candidate is revealed (reflecting the fact that for none is the moderate candidate a least preferred candidate). Risk-seeking voters make more errors than risk-averse voters (reflecting perhaps that the subjects are risk-averse in the monetary payoffs). Moderate voters are significantly more likely to vote for their least preference, but less so when the moderate candidate is revealed. This occurs because both the liberal and conservative candidates are moderate voters' least preferred and thus moderates are randomly more likely to vote for their least preferred candidate than the other voters but less so if the moderate, their preferred candidate, is revealed.

Conclusion: Sequential versus Simultaneous Voting

In summary, our experimental results provide evidence that:

- In simultaneous voting elections, voters generally choose as predicted and revealed candidates have a higher probability of winning than unrevealed candidates. However, voters show a tendency toward risk aversion in the monetary payoffs.
- Candidates revealed early are less likely to win in sequential voting than in simultaneous voting.
- The moderate candidate is more likely to win in simultaneous voting when voters know her identity, but more likely to win in sequential voting when her identity is less well known in the beginning.
- Early voters generally choose informatively.
- Later voters, when α is high (voters are risk-averse) and they know horse-race information by voter type, do infer information from early outcomes and choose their least preferred candidate less often than voters in simultaneous voting elections or early voters.

Our results suggest that sequential voting can allow later voters to make informed decisions but that this depends crucially on the detail of the information they have about early outcomes and the degree of risk aversion. Recall that both risk-seeking voters and a lack of detail about early balloting significantly decrease the probability that the moderate candidate wins. These results combined with our analysis of later voters' choices suggest that the probability that the moderate candidate wins is closely related to the ability of later voters to infer information from early balloting. *If later voters have detailed information about early balloting results and are risk-averse, then sequential voting is more likely to lead to more informed choices by later voters and, as a consequence, more wins for the moderate candidate.*

Our analysis suggests that sequential voting as in drawn-out primaries and early and mail-in balloting can be advantageous under limited circumstances—later voters can learn from early choices, and moderates can be more likely to win when not well-known. Does this mean that sequential voting elections are definitely superior to simultaneous voting elections? If the answer is yes, then why did states race to front-load their primaries in 1996? Why are states so worried about early voters dominating the process? Can early voters, who may not be representative, have an undue influence? Is this likely? And does the disadvantage of sequential voting outweigh the advantages? We turn to these questions in the next chapter.

CHAPTER 7

Representativeness of Early Voters and Sequential Voting Outcomes

The Importance of Representativeness

As noted, the downside of drawn-out primaries (sequential voting) is the potential disproportionate influence wielded by unrepresentative early voters. This is also one of the downsides of mail-in and early balloting. In both cases policymakers have argued against sequential voting election processes because unrepresentative early voters may have a greater weight in deciding the outcome. This was one of the principal reasons, as discussed in chapter 1, for the institution of a single federal election day for presidential selection in 1845 and for selection of congressional members in 1872.

In presidential primaries, as reviewed in chapter 2, ample evidence exists that voters in early states are not representative of the electorate at large. Voters in New Hampshire, in particular, have more extreme preferences than voters in other states, as documented by Erikson, Wright, and McIver 1993 and Keeter and Zukin 1983. Palmer contends: "Clearly, the question of the representative quality of a New Hampshire primary lies at the heart of the continuing controversy over its elevated electoral status" (1997, 48). Many in the popular media have repeatedly expressed concern that presidential nominations are highly contingent on performance in early states that may not be representative of the nations' voting preferences, that is, more extremely conservative or liberal. One of the reasons that many states are moving to front-loaded primaries is because of beliefs that early voters are influencing to a great extent the selection of presidential nominees and that later voters, like California in 1996, vote after the contest is virtually decided. Consequently, states have been jockeying since 1996 to be earlier in the 2000 selection process.[1]

In chapter 3, we found that in mail-in and early voting, voters who go to the polls early tend to be more partisan than later voters (Stein 1998). Oliver 1996 found that absentee voters are more likely to be Republican, although research on early voting in Texas has not shown a partisan bias. Berinsky, Burns, and Traugott 1998 found that, in Oregon, early voters were more likely to be resource-rich and long-term residents. Early voters typically are different from later voters—either in presidential primaries or in mail-in and early balloting elections. Does this mean that these voters can have a greater influence on election outcomes? Does the representativeness of early voters matter? We examine the effect of differences in representativeness of early voters in this chapter.

Does Representativeness Matter?

Measuring the Effect of Representativeness

As mentioned in chapter 6, we measure the effect of representativeness of early voters on outcomes in sequential voting by conducting two types of sequential voting elections, Sequential 1 (representative early voters manipulation) and Sequential 2 (nonrepresentative early voters manipulation). In Sequential 1, voter types are equally distributed across early and later voting groups—in each voting group there are 5 liberal voters, 2 moderate voters, and 5 conservative voters. In Sequential 2, voter types are unequally distributed across early and later voting groups—in group A (early voters) there are 10 liberals and 2 moderates, and in group B (later voters) there are 10 conservatives and 2 moderates. Tables 7.1 and 7.2 summarize how voter types are distributed in the two treatments and the sequential voting treatments were distributed by representativeness as well as risk aversion and information, respectively. In Sequential 2, since early voters are predominantly liberals, does this mean that the liberal candidate is more likely to win? More likely than in Sequential 1? Or in simultaneous voting elections?

TABLE 7.1.   Distribution of Voter Types in Sequential Voting Treatments

| | Sequential 1 (Representative Treatment) | | Sequential 2 (Nonrepresentative Treatment) | |
	Group A (Early Voters)	Group B (Later Voters)	Group A (Early Voters)	Group B (Later Voters)
Type 1 (liberals)	5	5	10	0
Type 2 (moderates)	2	2	2	2
Type 3 (conservatives)	5	5	0	10

TABLE 7.2. Summary of Experimental Design by Representativeness, Information, and Risk Aversion

	Nonrepresentative Sequential Voting Treatments		Representative Sequential Voting Treatments		
	High Information (Early Outcomes Told to Later Voters by Early Voter Type)	Low Information (Early Outcomes Told to Later Voters in Aggregate Only)	High Information (Early Outcomes Told to Later Voters by Early Voter Type)	Low Information (Early Outcomes Told to Later Voters in Aggregate Only)	Totals
High α (risk-averse voters)	25 elections with 24 subjects each = 600 voting decisions	25 elections 24 subjects = 600	25 elections 24 subjects = 600	25 elections 24 subjects = 600	100 elections 24 subjects = 2,400
Low α (risk-seeking voters)	25 elections with 24 subjects each = 600 voting decisions	25 elections 24 subjects = 600	25 elections 24 subjects = 600	25 elections 24 subjects = 600	100 elections 24 subjects = 2,400
Totals	50 elections with 24 subjects each = 1,200 voting decisions	50 elections 24 subjects = 1,200	50 elections 24 subjects = 1,200	50 elections 24 subjects = 1,200	200 elections 24 subjects = 4,800

Representativeness and Outcomes: Theoretical Predictions

In chapter 5, we discussed how both sincere and strategic voting equilibria are possible in sequential voting elections when later voters are able to learn from early balloting. Do our predictions change when we examine choices in Sequential 2 in which voter preferences are asymmetrically distributed (early voters are not representative of the electorate)? In Sequential 2 if the liberal candidate is revealed to early voters, we expect him to receive 10 votes from the early-liberal voters and the two early-moderate voters to randomize between the liberal and conservative candidates. This can give the liberal candidate a strong electoral advantage. Can the liberal candidate turn this advantage into a momentum-like effect on later voters, resulting in electoral victory?

Not necessarily. When later voters are able to learn from the horse-race information of early balloting, we expect that the nonrepresentative early voters do not necessarily increase the likelihood of the liberal candidate winning. When later voters can learn the identity of all three candidates from the outcome of early choices and the information they have, then the advantages that the liberal candidate may receive in early balloting is mitigated. This is more likely when voters are risk-averse. We would also expect that when early voters are nonrepresentative (as in Sequential 2), it will be easier for later voters to learn from the outcome of early choices. That is, there is less of a difference between the high and low information manipulations in Sequential 2 as compared with Sequential 1. Because of the increased likelihood that later voters can learn from early balloting, nonrepresentativeness can be lessened.

However, to the extent that later voters cannot learn from early choices, nonrepresentative early voters may have an undue influence on electoral outcomes. We state this possibility as Hypothesis 9 below. We test it against the null hypothesis, Hypothesis 0_f:

HYPOTHESIS 9. *Candidates preferred by liberal voters are more likely to win in Sequential 2 elections (nonrepresentative early voters manipulation) than in Sequential 1 elections (representative early voters manipulation).*

HYPOTHESIS 0_f. *Candidates preferred by liberal voters are no more likely to win in Sequential 2 elections (nonrepresentative early voters manipulation) than in Sequential 1 elections (representative early voters manipulation).*

Representativeness and Outcomes: Experimental Evidence

First, we consider whether the likelihood of winning by candidates revealed to early voters varies between Sequential 1 (representative early voters) and Sequential 2 (nonrepresentative early voters). A comparison-of-means test shows that there is no significant difference in the percentages of wins by first candidates revealed in the two treatments.[2] Yet, this evidence does not tell us whether the liberal candidate is more likely to win if revealed to early voters—which is a more precise test of Hypothesis 9. Table 7.3 presents comparison-of-means tests for the number of wins by candidates revealed to early voters in Sequential 2 (nonrepresentative early voters manipulation) elections versus Sequential 1 (representative early voters manipulation) elections by candidate type. The liberal candidate wins significantly more when revealed to early voters in Sequential 2 than Sequential 1, and the moderate and conservative candidates both win significantly less when revealed to early voters in Sequential 2 than Sequential 1. Thus, when early voters are told the identity of their first preference, that candidate is more likely to win and the representativeness of group A voters appears to matter.

Yet, the conclusion that the early voters have a disproportionate influence should be qualified. When the conservative candidate is revealed to later voters (the first preference of the majority of later voters in Sequential 2) he is much more likely to win.[3] Hence, the advantage of early voters in Sequential 2 crucially depends on the information that later voters have and whether early vot-

TABLE 7.3. Comparison-of-Means Tests of the Percentage of Wins by Candidates Revealed to Group A in Sequential 2 versus Sequential 1 by Candidate Type

	x (Liberal Candidate) Revealed to Group A (Early Voters)	*y* (Moderate Candidate) Revealed to Group A (Early Voters)	*z* (Conservative Candidate) Revealed to Group A (Early Voters)
Observations in Sequential 2 (nonrepresentative early voters)	33	38	29
Observations in Sequential 1 (representative early voters)	30	39	31
Mean Difference (Seq. 2 − Seq. 1)	0.31	−0.16	−0.43
Std. Error	0.10	0.09	0.09
t-statistic	2.99	−1.83	−4.65

Note: Ties are coded as 0.5.

ers can identify which candidate is their first preference. When early voters can identify their first preference (the liberal candidate), and later voters are not told the identity of their first preference (the conservative candidate), the liberal candidate is much more likely to win in Sequential 2.[4]

In order to control for the possible combined effects of the variables in the analysis, we report logit estimates of the probability that the liberal candidate wins in table D3 in appendix D.[5] In table 7.4, we summarize the effects of the various treatments on the predicted probability of the liberal candidate winning election. First, we find that when the liberal candidate is revealed to early voters, she is much more likely to win when voters are nonrepresentative (i.e., liberals dominate early voters) than when voters are representative regardless of whether voters are risk-averse or whether later voters have detailed information on early balloting. For example, when early voters are representative, risk-averse, and later voters have detailed information, the liberal candidate is predicted to win 41 percent of the time when revealed to early voters. But if these same early voters are nonrepresentative, the liberal candidate is predicted to win 83 percent of the time! Liberal candidates in this case do appear to have a strong momentum-like effect.

In contrast, if the conservative candidate is revealed to early voters, early voters are not predicted to have the same effect on the outcome, the liberal candidate favored by early voters is predicted to be less likely to win (with risk-averse voters and later voters with detailed information the liberal candidate is

TABLE 7.4.   Predicted Probability of Liberal Candidate Winning Election in Sequential Voting Elections (in Percentages)

		Representative Early Voters		Nonrepresentative Early Voters	
		High Information	Low Information	High Information	Low Information
High α (risk-averse voters)	Liberal candidate revealed to early voters	41	53	83	89
	Conservative candidate revealed to early voters	17	25	11	16
	Moderate candidate revealed to early voters	1	1	0	1
Low α (risk-seeking voters)	Liberal candidate revealed to early voters	55	66	90	93
	Conservative candidate revealed to early voters	27	37	17	26
	Moderate candidate revealed to early voters	1	2	1	1

Note: Period = 25, calculated using values in table D.3.

predicted to win 17 percent of the time with representative early voters, but only 11 percent with nonrepresentative early voters). When the moderate candidate is revealed to early voters, representativeness of early voters has only a negligible effect on the likelihood of the liberal candidate winning (with risk-averse voters and later voters with detailed information the liberal candidate is predicted to win 1 percent of the time with representative early voters, but 0 percent of the time with nonrepresentative early voters). Thus, the liberal candidate wins more often when early voters are less representative only when he is revealed to them. Having risk-seeking voters or later voters with low information also increases the predicted probability that the liberal candidate wins. In fact, when voters are nonrepresentative and risk-seeking, and later voters do not have detailed information on early voter choices, if the liberal candidate is revealed to nonrepresentative early voters, she is predicted to win almost all the elections, *93 percent,* of the time, a huge momentum-like effect.

In conclusion, *representativeness of early voters* matters—*when the candidate favored by nonrepresentative early voters is known to them, that candidate is more likely to win*. There are reasons to suspect that this is likely—that voters are more likely to know more about candidates who are closer to them ideologically. Thus, the empirical evidence suggests that nonrepresentative early voters can bias electoral outcomes in their favor.

Nonrepresentative Early Voting versus Simultaneous Voting Elections

Our analysis shows that it is possible that nonrepresentative early voters can lead to a bias in the electoral outcomes in drawn-out primaries or mail-in and early balloting elections (sequential voting elections) when these voters know which of the three candidates they most prefer. However, our analysis in the previous chapter also shows that sequential voting in general compared to simultaneous voting can lead to more wins by the moderate, the Condorcet winner, in some circumstances: when α is high (voters are risk-averse), the moderate candidate is revealed to early voters, and the moderate candidate is not the well-known candidate in simultaneous voting elections. Does this advantage of drawn-out primaries and mail-in and early balloting outweigh the disadvantage when early voters are nonrepresentative?

In order to answer this question, we estimated logits similar to that reported in table D1, where we compared the likelihood of the moderate candidate winning in simultaneous voting elections with sequential voting elections by the representativeness of early voters. The results of these estimations are presented in table D3 in appendix D. The effects of representativeness on the resulting predicted probabilities of the moderate candidate winning are presented in table 7.5. We find very similar results when we compare nonrepresentative sequential voting with simultaneous voting as when we compare representative sequential voting with simultaneous voting. Nonrepresentative early voters lead to a somewhat slightly increased likelihood that the moderate candidate will win (about a 1 percent increase in probability for all cases). *Hence, surprisingly, when early voters in sequential voting are nonrepresentative, sequential voting's advantage over simultaneous voting is greater rather than less, however the difference is only about 1 percent.*

Representativeness and Learning by Voting

We argued that theoretically later voters should be able to learn more from nonrepresentative early voters than from representative ones. That is, when early

TABLE 7.5. Predicted Probability of Moderate Candidate Winning by Sequential Voting Type (in percentages)

Nonrepresentative Sequential Voting

	Simultaneous Voting		Moderate Not Revealed		Moderate Revealed to Early Voters		Moderate Revealed to Later Voters	
	Liberal or Conservative Candidate Revealed	Moderate Candidate Revealed	High Information	Low Information	High Information	Low Information	High Information	Low Information
High α (risk-averse voters)	29	97	61	40	94	88	65	44
Low α (risk-seeking voters)	18	95	46	27	90	80	51	31

Representative Sequential Voting

	Simultaneous Voting		Moderate Not Revealed		Moderate Revealed to Early Voters		Moderate Revealed to Later Voters	
	Liberal or Conservative Candidate Revealed	Moderate Candidate Revealed	High Information	Low Information	High Information	Low Information	High Information	Low Information
High α (risk-averse voters)	29	97	60	39	94	87	64	43
Low α (risk-seeking voters)	18	95	45	26	90	79	49	30

Note: Period = 25, calculated using table D4 values.

TABLE 7.6. **Predicted Probability Voter Chooses Least Preferred Candidate (in percentages)**

| | Simultaneous and Early Voters | | Later Voter in Sequential Voting with Nonrepresentative Early Voters | | Later Voter in Sequential Voting with Representative Early Voters | | | |
| | | | | | Extreme Candidate Revealed to Voter | | Moderate Candidate Revealed to Voter | |
	Extreme Candidate Revealed to Voter	Moderate Candidate Revealed to Voter	Extreme Candidate Revealed to Voter	Moderate Candidate Revealed to Voter	High Information	Low Information	High Information	Low Information
High α (risk-averse voter) Moderate vote	36	5	42	7	16	42	2	7
Extreme voter	15	10	2	12	0	2	3	12
Low α (risk-seeking voter) Moderate voter	52	10	58	12	26	58	3	12
Extreme voter	3	17	4	21	1	4	6	21

Note: Period = 25, calculated using values in table D5.

voters are nonrepresentative their choices should be easier to understand and use as an information source. But our result, that nonrepresentative voters can influence the outcome of elections, suggests that learning may not be occurring in these sequential voting elections. To determine if nonrepresentative early voters increase or decrease the learning by later voters, we estimate a logit similar to the one reported in table D2—where we estimate the predicted probability that a voter chooses her least preferred candidate controlling for the representativeness of early voters. This logit is reported in table D4 in appendix D.

Table 7.6 summarizes the results of this estimation for the predicted probability that a voter will choose her least preferred candidate as a function of the different variables. First, there is little difference in the predicted mistakes of later voters by the detail of information provided them when early voters are nonrepresentative; variables measuring this effect were insignificant. This is what we expect. However, although detail of information is not significant, later voters, when early voters are nonrepresentative, are surprisingly likely to make more mistakes and vote for their least preferred candidates more often than when early voters are representative. This is not what we expect. The mistakes made are predicted, in fact, to be higher for this group of voters as compared to both simultaneous and early voters and later sequential voters in the representative detailed information treatment. Later voters in the nonrepresentative treatment are predicted to make almost the same number of mistakes as later voters in the representative sequential voting treatment who do not have detailed information on early voting outcomes. *Nonrepresentativeness does not increase the ability of later voters to learn and, as with a lack of detailed information on representative early voters' choices, appears to make voters less informed.*

The Effects of Representativeness: A Summary

Nonrepresentative early voters do appear to be able to influence outcomes significantly if they know who their favored candidates are—their favored candidates (when known) are more likely to win than when early voters are representative. Their candidate's early success can seem to have a momentum-like effect. Later voters do not appear to learn as much from nonrepresentative early voters' choices as from detailed information about representative early voters' choices. However, when early voters are nonrepresentative, there is a slight increase in the probability that moderate candidates win.

In the next chapter, we review these results and the rest of our analysis and their implications for real-world electoral systems. We also discuss avenues for future research on simultaneous and sequential voting elections.

CHAPTER 8

Ordering Voters in Future Elections—
Implications of Our Research for
Presidential Primaries and Mail
and Mall Voting

What Have We Learned?

Should We Worry about Nonrepresentative Early Voters?

We begin our summary of results with the last analysis—our study of the effects of representativeness of early voters. In chapter 1, we found that the issue of representativeness is one of the major factors leading to the establishment of a uniform federal election day for the selection of presidents and members of Congress. Recently, in *Foster v. Love* (1998), the Supreme Court supported the right of Congress to require that voting take place simultaneously on a single federal election day. In chapter 2, we discussed how in presidential primaries concerns of policymakers that early states with nonrepresentative voters have an undue influence have led to the front-loading of presidential primaries in a short period and to calls for a national presidential primary or a set of regional primaries. In chapter 3, we reviewed the evidence that suggests that in early and mail-in balloting, early voters are different from later ones. We noted that some policymakers are worried that these systems may lead to a greater influence for early nonrepresentative voters on election outcomes.

In chapter 7 we investigated whether these concerns are justified—can nonrepresentative early voters have a disproportionate influence on the election outcome? We found that the influence of nonrepresentative early voters depends on the knowledge they have about the candidates' policy positions. When early voters are not representative of the electorate at large and can identify their most preferred candidate, that candidate has a *much* greater likelihood of winning. Moreover, later voters do not appear to learn from nonrepresentative early voters. These results suggest that nonrepresentative early voters can have negative consequences. *When voter information is asymmetrically distributed across voters, the representativeness of early voters can affect the electoral out-*

come. Thus, policymakers and state legislators who advocate front-loading of
presidential primaries to increase their influence on the election outcome seem
justified. Furthermore, concerns about early and mail-in balloting leading to
more influence by early voters are also justified.

Can Later Voters Learn in Sequential Voting?

In chapters 1 and 2 we examined the belief of some policymakers that in sequential voting elections (as in drawn-out presidential primaries) later voters
can learn during the sequential voting process. Policymakers see simultaneous
voting elections as advantaging well-known candidates—that the sequential
voting process can allow a previously unknown candidate to build support
among voters as information is aggregated during the electoral process. Yet,
later voters generally receive horse-race information from early choices—and
it is an open question as to how useful such information can be. Can later voters learn from horse-race results of early balloting?

The concerns about information effects in mail-in and early balloting systems are slightly different. Some critics of mail-in and early balloting find it
problematic that voters choosing at different points in the electoral process may
have different degrees of information and the resulting electoral outcomes will
be affected, as discussed in chapters 1 and 3. The situation is probably more
similar to our low information experimental treatment since, currently, information on early voter choices is not publicized before later voters choose—but
potentially this information could be provided via public opinion polls. As
noted in chapter 1, members of the news media recognize that they could make
estimates of early and mail-in choices. If so, this information may have an effect on later voter choices. Therefore, it is important to assess whether later voters may use horse-race information on early voter balloting and the potential
influence such information may have.

In chapter 6, we investigate the extent that later voters use horse-race information from early choices and the effects such information may have on
electoral outcomes and later voting behavior. We find evidence that in sequential voting later voters can use horse-race information from early choices to infer information about the candidates and thus make voting decisions that more
accurately reflect their preferences. That is, later voters in sequential voting
elections choose their least preferred candidates less often than voters in simultaneous voting elections or early voters in sequential voting elections when
α is high (voters are risk-averse) and later voters know the outcome of early
voting by voter type (high information manipulation). However, when α is low
(risk-seeking voters) or voters are not given information about the early voting
by voter type (low information manipulation), later voters appear less able to

infer information about the candidates from the electoral outcomes of early choices. Finally, when early voters are nonrepresentative, learning does not seem to occur even when later voters have detailed information and are risk-averse. Hence, if there is the possibility that voters are risk-averse, detailed information is available, and early voters are representative, then information aggregation in sequential voting is more likely. In conclusion, learning by voting in sequential voting elections can occur, but this depends on the detail of information provided to voters, voters' risk aversion levels, and the representativeness of early voters. *The argument that sequential voting as in drawn-out presidential primaries and mail-in and early balloting leads to learning by voting and more informed voter choices is supported only on a limited basis. Thus, learning by voting may occur, but only when the horse-race information provided to later voters is detailed.*

Are Winners in Sequential Voting Elections Different?

Does the learning that can take place advantage particular candidates? When later voters are able to use early voting information, and the moderate candidate would not be the well-known candidate in simultaneous voting, she is more likely to win in sequential than in simultaneous voting elections. The learning by voting can advantage the moderate candidate. *Since the moderate is the Condorcet winner and thus is preferred by a majority of the voters to either the liberal or conservative candidates in pairwise competitions, sequential voting, under some conditions, produces more desirable electoral outcomes than simultaneous voting if it is likely that the well-known candidate in simultaneous voting is not the Condorcet winner.* Our results indicate that where there is the possibility that one unknown is moderate (the Condorcet winner) and voters are risk-averse, sequential voting may allow voters to aggregate information about the distribution of candidate types through the electoral process and lead to a higher probability of that candidate winning than in simultaneous voting. *Sequential voting may, in this context, lead to the election of a Condorcet winner who might lose in simultaneous voting elections in which he or she is relatively unknown.*

In conclusion, policymakers who contend that drawn-out presidential primaries have an informational advantage are supported if later voters are given sufficient information about the outcome of voting in early states and the Condorcet winner or winners are unknown. Representativeness of early voters is most likely to be a concern in drawn-out presidential primaries and mail-in and early balloting systems when early voters know well their most preferred candidates and later voters are less able to identify the candidates (have less of their own independent information).

Implications of Our Results for Naturally Occurring Elections

Presidential Primaries in the Real World

Our analysis explains to a large extent why states have engaged in front-loading of presidential primaries—nonrepresentative early voters can have an influence on election outcomes. Our results also support policymakers who believe that drawn-out presidential primaries can have informational advantages—under certain conditions later voters can learn from early choices, and unknown candidates who are moderates (Condorcet winners) can be advantaged. It is important to reiterate the advantage gained from our experimental analysis over using naturally occurring data on presidential nomination contests. As discussed in chapters 1 and 2, only since approximately 1976 have presidential primaries dominated these nominations—leading to an extremely limited amount of variation in candidate and voter preference types. Our experimental work allows us to consider how representativeness matters in terms of cause and effect, how the degree of information available to later voters matters, and how the degree of voter risk aversion matters.

In chapters 2 and 4 we reviewed some of the other empirical and theoretical literature on presidential primaries. How does our analysis fit in with this research? First, our analysis provides micro-level support for the macro-level phenomenon of momentum and some explanations as to when momentum is likely to have an effect and when not. We find some strong evidence of a momentum-like effect when early voters are nonrepresentative and have knowledge of their most preferred candidate. In these cases, their most preferred candidate is significantly more likely to win election, building on her early success with nonrepresentative early voters. We also find some support for momentum-like outcomes even when early voters are representative. That is, if the moderate candidate is known to early representative voters, she is more likely to win election than any of the other candidates. Early voter choices and knowledge do seem, in the laboratory, to have an effect on the outcome of the election, whether these voters are representative or not.

We also find some evidence of Bayesian updating by our subjects in the experiment when they are provided with detailed information about early voter choices. Later voters, with detailed information, are more likely to learn and make fewer errors. Learning in this fashion is more likely when voters are risk-averse, which also supports a Bayesian interpretation of voter use of information.

Mail and Mall Voting

Our investigation, similarly, provides useful information for research on early and mail-in balloting. Concerns that nonrepresentative early and mail-in voters may have an undue influence are supported by our results. The use of early and mail-in balloting is increasing, as outlined in chapter 3. Yet, only in the past decade have there been statewide elections with early voting, and only in a few states. As with presidential primaries, there is an extremely limited amount of variation in candidate and voter preference types to evaluate these systems empirically using naturally occurring data. Experimental investigation of electoral systems that are proposed but only used to a limited extent can have critical advantages. That is, if we restrict our analysis of how different electoral institutions work to naturally occurring data then we experiment with our own governmental choices—we experiment in selecting election winners. Laboratory elections can provide empirical evaluations that investigate with a wider variety of preference configurations and information levels than available from naturally occurring elections, and they also have a lower potential cost for society. Rather than experimenting in real elections with real candidates, laboratory elections can provide useful information about how different electoral institutions work without the potential effect on the actual real-world election outcomes!

Implications of Our Results for Future Research

Strategic Candidates

While the summary of our results presented above emphasizes what we have learned through our study of learning by voting in elections, our model and experimental analysis does leave and suggest a number of questions for future research—both experimental and nonexperimental. As the work of Aldrich 1980a,b and Strumpf 1997 highlights (reviewed in chapter 4), there are important strategic considerations for candidates when voting is sequential that we, of course, have ignored in our theoretical and empirical analysis. In presidential primaries, candidates may enter and exit during the nomination process—this should be considered in evaluating sequential versus simultaneous voting systems. Finally, presidential candidates, as history shows (and we noted in chapter 2), have historically been involved in the scheduling game between the states. For example, New Jersey presidential candidate Bill Bradley has attempted to get his state to reschedule their primary from June to March 2000 to help his candidacy.[1]

Furthermore, when electoral outcomes depend on voter information and the representativeness of early voters, this is no doubt likely to influence candidate campaigning and choices in reaching voters. Analysts of mail-in and early balloting systems suggest that these elections have become multistage affairs where candidates find they need to campaign to different sets of voters—

early and late. In chapter 1, we noted how Washington state congressman Brian Baird learned in 1996 that ignoring early voters can result in an election lost. But he did not give up. Romano 1998 reports that he ran again for office in 1998:

> The 42-year-old psychologist spent $1.6 million on his 1998 race, nearly $1 million more than in 1996, and much of it went toward targeting early mail voters. His campaign telephones about 100,000 potential absentee voters, sent them applications and made three early literature drops to reach them. Baird himself made a big show of voting-by-mail 12 days early, rather than on Election Day. In the end, an extraordinary 54 percent of his district voted by mail, and this time Baird won handily. But it wasn't easy, or cheap. Considering the primary as well as the general election, Baird said, 'we essentially had to run four campaigns to reach everyone.'

Ideally, our model and empirical work should allow for such strategic behavior.

Money

Another important extension of our model would be to incorporate more explicitly the influence of campaign expenditures on voter choices. Campaign spending limitations similarly may affect candidates more severely in elections with early and late voting, as spending to mobilize and convey information to early voters becomes as important as mobilization and information conveyance to later voters. In fact, mobilizing early voters may become even more important since these voters are more likely to be partisans and their votes more sure bets for some candidates. How do constraints on campaign spending affect the types of candidates who run, the information that voters have, and the choices that voters make in sequential voting elections? These issues are vital for understanding how elections work in the current environment, and we hope that future research can examine the interaction between campaign spending and voting order.

Turnout

In chapter 3 we discussed how one of the perceived advantages of mail-in and early balloting is an increase in political participation. Yet, empirical evidence from the existing experience with these elections suggests that while turnout may increase, it increases mainly among voters who would normally vote but find it more convenient to vote early. The evidence suggests that the increase in turnout is due to a stability in the turnout of partisan voters already motivated, whose turnout may be more random if elections were restricted to a single day.

Moreover, we discussed the potential negative effect of mail-in and early balloting on turnout of later voters in elections. In our experiments, we did not allow voters to abstain. Future research should consider these possible turnout effects.

Fraud, the Secret Ballot, and Turnout

One argument against early and mail-in balloting is that these procedures are less easy to control, allowing for a greater chance of fraud in elections. Surely the fact that the Miami mayoral election of 1997 had to be reheld because of fraudulent absentee ballots suggests that these concerns may not be unfounded.[2] Romano 1998 points out that the "motor voter" bill that requires states to allow mail-in voter registration without any form of identification may lead to a situation that "allows ineligible—and even nonexistent—voters to get on the rolls."

Moreover, some early and all mail-in ballots have an additional feature—they are not necessarily secret ballots. As Romano further observes: "The polling booth also guarantees privacy for voters. But when a person is filling out a ballot at home, they could be subject to intimidation, mail balloting critics say. 'It could become difficult or uncomfortable for a person to cast a different vote than her family. And how do we protect the elderly from pressure?' asked an adviser to a campaign that relied heavily on mail balloting." Some states are considering allowing Internet voting procedures (California and Florida, for example). Will voting over the Internet result in significantly less public voting? Heckelman 1995 argues that the secret ballot prevented bribery of voters, which was common in the nineteenth century before the passage of secret ballot laws. Bribery was no longer practical because there was no way to assure that a voter had chosen as desired. Heckelman estimates that with the introduction of secret ballots as much as 7 percent of turnout decreased because of a reduction in bribery.[3]

It seems straightforward that if early and mail-in ballots are more easily manipulated through fraud that fraud will be more likely in these systems. However, making voting a less private act may increase legitimate turnout. If the act of voting is a function of the efforts of groups of like-minded voters to mobilize participation through social incentives, as argued in chapter 3, then when the act of voting is less private, mobilization of voters may increase. At what point is this mobilization a "bribe" of an uninterested voter for a candidate or party she does not support or the legitimate act of a voter convinced to cast a vote she would benefit from as a group? Making voting more public makes it more difficult to determine the difference. Future experiments which make acts of voting more public and mobilization efforts are allowed may help provide answers as to the effects of social voting on turnout and election outcomes.

States, Parties, and the Federal Government

The histories of presidential primaries and mail-in and early balloting show a complicated system of mixed party, state, and federal rules governing election processes. It is no surprise that this has led to conflicts between governments and party officials, and ultimately to court challenges to state laws regulating participation in primaries and early and mail-in balloting. Our attention in this book has been to take the existing processes as given and to consider voter choices within these electoral systems. Yet, the intricate relationship between state, party, and federal authority in scheduling when voters choose, we believe, should be investigated. What are the advantages and disadvantages of the diversity in authority over electoral processes? Currently there is much new formal research on how federated governments maintain stability (Cremer and Palfrey 1999). Applying some of this research to electoral laws should help increase our understanding of why such complexity of authority may exist in electoral processes.

A Final Word

While our results provide a large data set for analysis, these empirical results depend on the assumptions we make about voter preferences; available candidate information, and also on the way we have designed our experiments. Future research should investigate different candidate choices and differences in voter perceptions. We hope that our work will spur *much* future theoretical and empirical research—both experimental and nonexperimental—comparing sequential and simultaneous voting.

Formal Models, Experiments, and Elections

How Formal Models Work

Assumptions in Formal Models

A formal model is a model that has explicitly stated assumptions about the "real world" from which predictions are derived.[1] However, because it is a model, by definition some of the assumptions are false or unverifiable. That is, the model abstracts from reality, and the assumptions are the explicitly stated details of the abstraction. Nonformal models, in contrast, do not explicitly state how the model abstracts from reality, although such abstractions and idealizations are implicit in nonformal theories. The advantage of a formal model is that these abstractions and idealizations are explicit, and the predictions can be traced and logically deduced from the assumptions.

When we empirically evaluate a formal model's predictions we learn not only whether the prediction is supported but we also learn about the support for our assumptions in the real world. We can use the empirical evaluation to revise the theory and increase our understanding of how the theory works. Theories and conjectures based on nonformal models when empirically evaluated cannot tell us much about the support for their underlying assumptions since these are unknown. Of course, formal models are more easily criticized than nonformal models, since the explicitness of the assumptions allows a critic the opportunity to argue that the model is problematic because its assumptions are false. This criticism by itself, however, is vacuous since all models, whether formal or nonformal, are not the same as the naturally occurring environment and thus have either explicit or implicit false assumptions. Criticism of a formal model's assumptions makes sense if the critic can show that the results of the model hinge crucially on a particular assumption that is likely to be false *and* that another theory performs better in empirical evaluation.

Choosing Assumptions in a Formal Model

Because they are so crucial in modeling, the assumptions in a formal model must be carefully chosen, chosen in order to capture the important aspects of the naturally occurring environment that the theorist is interested in while not making the model so complex as to be useless. Formal theoretical models face the same sort of design constraints as physical models of bridges, airplanes, buildings, and so forth. Suppose, for example, that we wanted to build a model of Central Park in New York City. We would need to decide what we are trying to explain or show with our model first. We might be interested in the flow of waters in the park. If so, then it would be important that we have actual water in our model and that the depth of the waterways be part of the model. On the other hand, if we are interested mainly in the visual beauty of the park, we could do without water and simply use a mirror or painted image to represent the water, ignoring the depth. Since our model is necessarily smaller than the actual park, there are details that we cannot fully represent. We may or may not have people or animal figures in our model, depending on what we plan to use our model to study or show. For example, suppose we want to understand how the park might be used for a concert. Then people figures might be quite useful. On the other hand, if our focus is on the landscape architectural beauty of the park, having people figures, especially at a concert, might interfere with our ability to understand how the park's landscape should best be shaped.

To see how formal models work in a similar way, consider the literature on the organizational structure of Congress. Researchers have used a number of formal models to understand how different aspects of the organizational structure works. For example, Baron and Ferejohn (1989) use a simple bargaining game where a number of players vote over proposals on how to divide a fixed sum to model legislative bargaining. In the model, a legislator is chosen to make a proposal on how to divide the sum, which is voted over by the entire legislature. If the proposal is rejected, then another legislator is given the option of making a proposal until a proposal is accepted. The model captures the pork barrel (distributive nature) of much legislation and the impact of proposal power on the outcomes of legislative bargaining.

Baron and Ferejohn examine how different rules on whether amendments can be made to the proposals affect the types of proposals that result. They show that a rule that prevents amendments (a closed rule) is likely to result in proposals where the proposer gets a larger share than a rule that allows amendments (an open rule). The model therefore yields the prediction that on redistributive legislation, legislative leadership is more likely to choose closed rules than open rules.

The model ignores many of the details of the actual U.S. Congress. The legislature is unicameral in the model. All legislation is redistributive in nature.

The roles of voters and elections are ignored. There are no interest groups, lobbyists, or campaign contributions. The legislature has no staff. The legislature is not constrained by potential presidential vetoes or judicial review. There is no bureaucracy necessary to implement policy. The model ignores these details in order to focus on one aspect of how legislative rules work in the Congress. Yet, it provides insight into the benefits to legislative leadership of control over amendments when legislation is redistributive. If all the ignored details were included in the model the theorist would be less able to see the connection between the type of legislation and the effect of the different institutional rules. Formal models make simplistic assumptions in order to provide clear and focused predictions, which often means that some details are ignored while others are emphasized—just as a physical model of Central Park designed to model the landscape beauty may not have the same people figures as a model designed to understand how concerts work in the park should have.

Assumptions in Our Model

Similarly, our model necessarily simplifies the electoral process substantially, both to allow for analytical predictions and to facilitate our experimental investigation. For example, our simple model has only three candidates, and candidates are not allowed to enter or exit the electoral process. We examine only a one-stage electoral contest. That is, in applying our model to the presidential primary process, we ignore differences in the ways primary elections select delegates and caucuses altogether (in some primaries, delegates are allocated according to candidate vote shares while in others the delegates are allocated on a winner-take-all basis). Our simple model assumes that all delegates are allocated on a proportional basis. We do not model state and local elections that may influence presidential primary voting. We do not model the general election process or the electoral college. Analogously, our model vastly simplifies the voting process of mail-in or early balloting by ignoring pre–general election primaries and other factors that affect candidate decisions. We do not endogenize turnout and other participation decisions or the timing of voting.

Nevertheless, we believe that our model captures some of the more salient features of presidential primaries and other elections with sequential voting that concern policymakers; this allows us to focus on the effects of these features on electoral outcomes and voting behavior. We discuss these assumptions and our justifications for them in more detail in the subsequent chapters (in particular, see chap. 5). By explicitly making assumptions we can then derive predictions from the model about how simultaneous voting, as in a virtual national primary or standard single-day elections, may lead to different outcomes (different types of candidates elected) than sequential voting, as in drawn-out primaries or mail-in and early balloting elections, for a given set of candidates and voter preferences. We can consider how representativeness and information levels of early voters affect the outcomes in sequential voting by varying voter preference configurations and information.

Using a formal model allows us to examine how different features or aspects of presidential primaries and other sequential voting systems work. Just as models of Congress often ignore its bicameral nature in order to center on other particular characteristics such as the effects of proposal power or rules governing amendments, we simplify sequential voting so that we can focus our analysis on these important questions. While we are extremely interested in exploring candidate entry and exit in presidential primaries, differences in the way delegates are allocated, and other aspects of presidential primaries that we ignore, we do not examine these details in this book so that we can focus on the facets that we emphasize. Similarly we do not endogenize turnout or timing in mail-in and early balloting, important aspects of these elections. We see our model as an important first step in examining these questions and welcome extensions and generalizations of our model's assumptions. We hope that future work can incorporate and investigate these other features of presidential primaries and other sequential voting systems.

Laboratory Experiments and Formal Models

Problems in Empirically Evaluating Theory

Laboratory experiments are increasingly used to analyze the predictions of formal models. In many cases laboratory experiments allow a researcher to evaluate theory empirically in ways that are unavailable if the researcher is restricted to using only naturally occurring data. As noted, formal models often necessarily ignore details about the naturally occurring world. When we use naturally occurring data to evaluate these models empirically we have three choices: (1) resolve the model to incorporate these details, (2) take the model as-is and directly evaluate it using naturally occurring data, ignoring the overlooked details, or (3) take the model, make conjectures about how the omitted details might affect the predictions of the model, and add controls to the empirical analysis to evaluate these conjectures.[2]

Option 1 is attractive but misleadingly so. That is, formal models' advantage is that they provide predictions based on clear explicit assumptions. If the assumptions must be continually generalized the model becomes complex and the predictions less clear. Empirical evaluation becomes less useful. Our theoretical model, if generalized to incorporate entry and exit, general elections, state elections, turnout, and timing of balloting, will become more complex and hard to evaluate. Moreover, we may be making wrong choices in our modeling because we do not know whether our first choices are empirically supported. That is, based on early theoretical results alone without empirical evaluation we may focus in one direction over another. If we wait till our model is complex enough to handle all the things we can anticipate that exist in the naturally occurring world (something that is impossible at any rate), we may waste time that would be better used exploring a different direction in our theory.

Option 2, taking the model as-is and directly empirically evaluating it using naturally occurring data, ignoring the overlooked details, is a strong test of the theory. One errant observation suggests that the theory is not supported. Yet we fully expect errant observations since we *know* there are disconnects between the theory and the empirical world. Nevertheless, the empirical evaluation of a model under such strong conditions yields important information about which disconnects are significant and which are not.

The modal method for analyzing formal models is to choose option 3, taking the model, making conjectures about how the ignored details might affect the predictions of the model, and adding controls to the empirical analysis to evaluate these conjectures. Under option 3 our empirical evaluation is of the model *plus* our conjectures about the omitted details. It is not an independent evaluation of the model's predictions, and thus the empirical analysis cannot be seen as conclusive. We do not know if successful or unsuccessful empirical evaluations mean the model is independently supported or not because of the added conjectures. This is a major reason why multiple empirical evaluations, using a variety of methods, are useful.

Advantages of Laboratory Experiments

Laboratory experiments provide a unique method of choosing option 2 more effectively and providing empirical evaluation of formal models. That is, instead of making conjectures about how the omitted details matter and adding variables to empirical estimation to statistically control for these ignored features as in option 3, we use our experimental design to control for the omissions. For example, in the laboratory we can control the number of candidates such that they do not change when voters vote sequentially. We can have the votes counted as if delegates were chosen according to a proportionality rule rather than winner-take-all. We can control the timing and turnout decisions of voters. Thus, we use our design to allow us to conduct a strong test of the theory using option 2.

Laboratory experiments have other advantages in empirical analysis of formal models. Our use of experiments permits us to compare voting systems holding voters' preferences constant and to compare the effects of changes in the preference distributions of early voters upon electoral outcomes and voting behavior in sequential voting. If we were using naturally occurring data we would have to measure voter preferences over candidates, which can be difficult. We also would have to take the distribution of preferences given to us by the naturally occurring environment. If voters' preferences in early primary states, for instance, were not representative of the general population, we would not be able to force representative voters to move to these early primary states to evaluate empirically the effects of representativeness on the electoral outcomes or vice versa (nor could we force the states to reconfigure their primary schedule to fit our theoretical needs). We cannot conduct the comparative test using naturally occurring data. In the laboratory, we can make the financial payoffs from the electoral outcomes salient enough to induce voter preferences and thus explicitly empirically evaluate the effects of representativeness.

Similarly, if we want to compare virtual national primaries with more drawn-out primaries using naturally occurring elections, we are forced to conduct a historical comparison where the number and types of candidates vary, voter preferences are different, and other relevant features of the primary election process are distinct. The information voters have about the candidates and the way in which this information is provided can differ over time. There are very few data points to use for such a comparison and far too many complicating factors that can explain the results. Most agree that presidential primaries have only dominated the nomination process since 1972; thus we have at best 14 data points, a number of which involved unchallenged incumbent presidents. By using laboratory experiments we can make that comparison holding constant the number and types of candidates, voter preferences, and the other features of the primary system.

We face comparable, although somewhat fewer, problems in empirical analyses of mail-in and early balloting. While many states are beginning to allow for increased mail-in and early balloting, their use is still quite limited. In chapter 3 we review the empirical evidence on mail-in and early voting—as we discuss, there are very few studies of individual-level choices in these elections, and our experiments can provide such data. Moreover, for a proposed new voting system, experiments can provide us with information on how that voting system could work in advance of use in naturally occurring elections where the effects on electoral outcomes might be significant for public policy. The cost of experimenting with different electoral procedures in terms of real-world effects can be substantially less!

In the laboratory, we can control the information voters have and how they are conveyed that information. We can conduct a large number of experimental elections, yielding a much bigger data set. In fact, we compile a rich and large data set (250 elections and 6,000 voting decisions) on the effects of these important aspects of simultaneous and sequential voting, data that are not available if we restrict our study to naturally occurring elections.

However, we see our experimental work not as a substitute for the study of naturally occurring elections, which include the many factors that we omit in our research, but as complementary to that research, providing additional and unique evidence on the effects of different voting institutions on electoral outcomes and voting behavior controlling some of the more difficult-to-measure variables in naturally occurring elections such as voter preferences and candidate types. Our research, of course, is only one step in the process of increasing our understanding of the effect of the order of voting on electoral outcomes and voting behavior and, we hope, will lead to more study that examines aspects of elections that we necessarily simplify.

Our Research Design and Causal Inference

The advantages of experiments in evaluating formal models in general leads us to the more general point that our research design, a combination of a formal model with experimental tests, is particularly suited to deal with the small *n* problem of research on presidential primaries and mail-in and early balloting. As King points out, research on the presidency suffers strongly from the fundamental problem of causal inference (in presidency research, the small *n* problem) that afflicts all empirical analysis of theory. King explains:

> For simplicity, consider the causal hypothesis that presidents who were once members of Congress veto legislation less frequently. The precise definition of this causal effect is as follows. Consider one president, say Jimmy Carter, and observe the number of veto orders he signs during his four years in office. Then take the same president, turn the clock and the world back to 1976, alter Jimmy Carter so that he is alike in all respects except that he served as a member of Congress, make everyone (but you!) forget the first experiment, and run the world a second time. The causal effect is then the difference between the number of vetoes from these two experiments. It should be obvious that one cannot *know* the causal effect even in theory, since one of the values required (the number of vetoes for each experiment) is always unobserved. (1993, 402)

We believe that in a number of ways our research design combining a formal model with experimental analysis allows us to lessen this fundamental problem significantly. First of all, we can, through our experiment, come extremely close to the theoretical design or running history in two directions at once. That is, our subjects are drawn randomly for each treatment from a common subject pool. Within each treatment, our subjects are randomly assigned preference types, and the candidate information is randomly chosen. Second, we are able to generate a large number of electoral outcomes so that we can examine how nomination procedure affects the type of candidate elected.

King argues that the common practice of using the president as the unit of analysis in presidency research is "extremely unlikely to yield reliable empirical conclusions" because the number of presidents available for statistical significance is far too few. He calculates that at least a number of centuries would need to pass before we would have enough observations even using all the former presidents as observations. A comparative study of the effect of drawn-out versus simultaneous primaries yields extremely fewer observations than just the number of presidents. King basically argues that the tradition of using the presidency as the unit of analysis should not continue. Our use of experiments allows us to yield data points that simply are not (and are unlikely to be) available if we restrict analysis to naturally occurring data. We can look at the type of candidate elected as a function of voting procedure.

Finally, and importantly, our research design also allows us better to follow King's advised solution to the president as unit of analysis problem. He suggests that "the solution is to look for ways of multiplying the number of observations—looking for additional observable implications of the same theory" and that we can increase the number of observations by looking "for observable implications of one's theory at other levels of aggregation" (1993, 406, 408). Formal models can provide predictions at multiple levels of aggregation. Our theory, for example, makes predictions about both the outcomes of the elections and the voting behavior of the subjects. Therefore, we are able to have large numbers of observations of voting choices as well as electoral outcomes.

Of course, studies with naturally occurring voting data on choices in presidential primaries and mail-in and early balloting can also be used. One advantage of our voting choice data is the ability that we have to vary the information the voters have on their candidate choices. In naturally occurring data the candidate choices and information available to all voters are subject to the same unit of analysis problem that occurs when the level of analysis is at a higher level of aggregation. That is, while moving to a lower level of aggregation in naturally occurring presidential primaries does expand the number of choices that one can examine, these choices are made in the context of a limited number of elections. In our experimental design we examine a wide variety of elections.

But most significantly, we believe that theories based on formal models are better suited for providing additional observable implications than theories based on nonformal models. We can take the formal model and derive additional predictions by changing the assumptions (essentially adding or loosening constraints in the model). We can "create" more observable implications of the theory in this fashion. In our work, for example, we examine how sequential voting varies depending on the information about candidates provided to later voters. The theory makes predictions about how the variation will affect the choices, and we can empirically evaluate these predictions.

Theories based on nonformal models are more limited in their ability to generate additional observable implications. That is, a nonformal model is a set of conjectures about reality. But because the basis from which the conjectures are derived is not formally stated, additional conjectures can add more implicit and untested assumptions, which may be inconsistent with the implicit assumptions underlying the original conjectures. The results, because researchers do not know whether the larger set of conjectures is internally consistent (if its underlying implicit assumptions are consistent), become highly problematic. Additional observable implications from formal models, since we know the assumptions underlying them, do not suffer from this potential problem. Additional implications of formal models are thus easier to provide than nonformal models and are more empirically useful than those of nonformal models. We thus believe that our research design, combining a formal model with experimental work, can be highly useful for studying questions such as presidential nomination procedures because they can tackle these important empirical problems that exist in such studies.

Our Formal Voting Model and Proofs of Propositions

The basics of our voting model are presented in Morton and Williams 1999. In this appendix we outline the model and provide proofs of the propositions. In our model we assume three types of voters indexed by: $i = 1, 2, 3$ and three candidates: x, y, and z. Voter i's utility over candidate j, u_{ij}, $j = x, y, z$, is described in table 4.1 in the text with type 1 as liberal voters, type 2 as moderates, type 3 as conservatives—candidate x as the liberal candidate, candidate y as the moderate, and candidate z as the conservative. We assume that $1 > \alpha > \frac{1}{16}$. A voter submits a vote vector, (v_x, v_y, v_z) where v_x is the number of votes cast for candidate x, and so on. Under our assumption of plurality rule, a voter can cast the following vote vectors: $(1,0,0)$, $(0,1,0)$, $(0,0,1)$. We do not allow for abstention in our analysis. Finally, define n_i as the proportion of type i voters. We assume that $n_1 = n_3 > n_2$.

We use the voting equilibrium concept described in Myerson and Weber 1993. Voting equilibria exist when voter perceptions of relatively close races are justified by the electoral outcome. A voter's vote can affect the election outcome only if two or more candidates are in a tie for first place in the election. How a voter then perceives the relative likelihood of the assorted "close races" should matter in the voter's ballot choice. As in Myerson and Weber, we assume the following:

1. Near-ties between two candidates are perceived to be much more likely than between three or more candidates.
2. p_{jk} is the "pivot" probability that candidates j and k are in a close race for first place. These pivot probabilities are assumed to satisfy the following ordering condition (assuming three candidates, j, k, h): if the votes cast for j are less than the votes cast for k, then $p_{jh} \leq \varepsilon p_{kh}$, where $0 \leq \varepsilon < 1$.
3. Voters' ballot choices maximize their expected utility.

Under these assumptions, then, voter i will choose a vote vector that maximizes:

$$\Sigma_{j=x,y,z} \, v_j \, \Sigma_{k=x,y,z \neq j} \, p_{jk}[u_{ij} - u_{ik}]$$

Following Myerson and Weber, it can be shown that the pivot probabilities can be rescaled to sum to one, and as ε goes to zero the rescaled pivot probabilities converge to a limit vector $\mathbf{q} = (q_{xy}, q_{xz}, q_{yz})$, which also sums to one. Note q_{jk} is then the rescaled pivot probability that candidates j and k are in a close race for first place. Myerson and Weber show that $q_{jk} > 0$ only if one of the following conditions holds (Theorem 2, Myerson and Weber):

1. Either candidates j and k are both in the set of likely winners
2. Or, either j or k is the unique likely winner and the other candidate has the second-highest predicted score.

Thus, the expected utility from voting for candidates more likely to be in close races for first place is higher than for other candidates. In our analysis, we restrict ourselves to symmetric equilibria, that is, equilibria in which identical voters have identical voting strategies. We assume that no one knowingly votes for their least preferred choices, which are at best weakly dominated strategies.

Proofs of Propositions

Proof of Propositions 1 and 4. For the purposes of the proof, assume that Orange's position is really x, Blue's position is y, Green's position is z, and $\alpha > 0.5$. Assume that Orange's position is revealed as x. In this case, voters of type 1 have a dominant strategy of always voting for Orange and voters of types 2 and 3 have a dominant strategy of always voting for any combination of Green and Blue. Only one possible symmetric voting equilibrium in pure strategies exists, that is, with $x \gg y \approx z$. The limit pivot probability vector that supports this equilibrium is $(q_{12}, q_{13}, q_{23}) = (0.5, 0.5, 0)$. Assume that Blue's position is revealed as y. In this case voters of all types have either a weakly dominant or dominant strategy of always voting for Blue, y is the expected winner, and z and x are expected to be tied for second place. Assume that Green's position is revealed as z. In this case voters of type 3 have the same options as voters of type 1 when Orange's position is revealed. If $\alpha \leq 0.5$ the analysis follows if x or z is revealed. If y is revealed and $\alpha < 0.5$ types 1 and 3 maximize expected utility by voting for an unrevealed candidate and if $\alpha = 0.5$, these voters should randomize in the two strategies (they will be indifferent). QED

Proof of Proposition 2. First assume that voting is not informative, that voters in group A use the same voting strategy regardless of which candidate has been revealed to them. Voting by group A is thus expected to be random and unrelated to the information acquired. Consider the possible cases. Assume that the candidate revealed to voters in group A is x, the candidate revealed to voters in group B is z, and $\alpha > 0.5$. Voters of type 1 in group A cannot be rational by randomizing their votes in this case since z will be the expected winner and x will be expected to be tied for second. Similarly, if z is revealed to voters in group A and x is revealed to voters in group B, voters of type 3 cannot be maximizing expected utility if they vote unrelated to their information since x will be the expected winner and z will be expected to be tied for second. Now suppose that y is revealed to voters in group A and z is revealed to voters in group B. Again, voting in group B will advantage z with y expected to be tied for second, which means that randomized voting in group A by both voters of types 1 and 2 would not be expected utility maximizing. Similarly if y is revealed to voters in group A and x is revealed to voters in group B, randomized voting by voters of types 2 and 3 is not expected utility maximizing since x will be advantaged and more likely to win with y expected to be tied for second. Finally, assume that x is revealed to voters in group A and y is revealed to voters in group B. Voters of type 1 in group A are not expected utility maximizing by not voting for x since x will be expected to be in a tie for second, and similar results hold if z is revealed to voters in group A and y is revealed to voters in group B. The results when $\alpha \leq 0.5$ straightforwardly follow.   QED

Proof of Proposition 3. Assume that x is revealed to voters in group A. They expect that group B voters will know the entire distribution of candidates. Since type 2 voters always have a dominant or weakly dominant strategy of voting for y regardless of the expected outcome of the election, votes of type 2 will find it rational to randomize between y and z. Type 3 voters have a weakly dominant or dominant strategy of voting for either y or z, depending on which of these two candidates is more likely to be in second place or tied for first in the election. Given that this is just as likely for either and that voting for candidate x is dominated for voters of type 3, voters of type 3 will also randomize between y and z. Finally, type 1 voters receive a higher expected utility from voting for x than taking the chance of the lottery between y and z. A similar analysis holds for when z is revealed to voters in group A. When y is revealed, again type 2 voters will vote for y since this is their weakly dominant or dominant strategy regardless of outcome. Both voters of types 1 and 3 also have a weakly dominant or dominant strategy of voting for y rather than taking the lottery between x and z since $\alpha > 0.5$.   QED

Proof of Proposition 5. Assume that x is revealed to group A. Type 1 voters of group A vote for x and types 2 and 3 randomize between y and z. Sincere voting equilibria are possible if the randomization from the votes in group A is such that sincere voting and the outcome of voting in group A leads to an expected outcome with either x and z in a tie for first place or one of the extremists is the expected winner and the other is expected to be in second place alone. Strategic voting equilibria are possible when voters of type 3 vote strategically for y and the randomization from the votes in group A is such that the expected outcome is either a tie between x and y or one is expected to be in first place and the other is expected to be in second place alone. Strategic voting equilibria are also possible in which voters of type 1 vote strategically for y and the randomization from the votes in group A is such that the expected outcome is either a tie between z and y or one is expected to be in first place and the other is expected to be in second place alone. Strategic voting equilibria are not possible in which both types 1 and 3 voters vote for y in group B, since if either x or z is expected to be in second place alone, that candidate's supporters maximize expected utility by voting sincerely, and if both extreme candidates are expected to be in a tie for second place, both candidates' supporters maximize expected utility by voting sincerely. Converse results hold if z is revealed to group A. If y is revealed to group A, then y is the expected winner in any equilibrium, and voting by group B members depends on expectations of which candidate will be in second place. If one extremist candidate is expected to be in second place alone, that candidate's supporters maximize expected utility by voting sincerely and the other extremist candidate's supporters maximize expected utility by voting strategically. If both extremists are expected to be in a tie for second place, both extremist supporters maximize expected utility by voting sincerely. QED

Experiment Instructions for Sequential Voting Elections

General. This is an experiment that examines voting behavior. The instructions are simple, and if you are careful and make good decisions you can earn a considerable amount of money. Your payoff depends on your decisions, but also on the decisions that other subjects make, and chance.

During the experiment you will participate in a series of elections. As in other elections, there will be voters who cast ballots for competing candidates. In the experiment you will play the role of voters. You will participate in a series of plurality elections. Plurality elections are elections in which there are more than two competing candidates. In this experiment there will be three candidates—we will call them Orange, Blue, and Green. The winner in a plurality election is simply the candidate who receives the most votes. In the case where candidates receive an equal share of the votes, the winner will be selected by a random draw. Your payoff in the experiment is tied directly to the winning candidate. Each of you will be given a payoff schedule that assigns a monetary amount to each of the three candidates. You will receive the monetary amount associated with the winning candidate.

Payoffs. Since you are here primarily for the money involved, let me explain your payoffs in more detail now. Each of you will have a payoff schedule that associates a monetary amount with each of the three candidates. For example, to you, the Orange candidate might be worth one dollar, while the Blue candidate might be worth 50 cents and the Green candidate might be worth 25 cents. In this case, the Orange candidate yields the higher payoff. However, for some voters the monetary amounts associated with each candidate might differ. Hence, the Orange candidate might yield a higher payoff for some voters, while the Blue candidate might yield a higher payoff for other voters. It is also possible for two or more candidates to be associated with the same payoff. Again, your payoff is based on the monetary amount assigned to the winning candidate. Assume that the monetary amount associated with the Orange candidate is one dollar and the monetary amount associated with the Green candidate is 50 cents. Consequently, even though the monetary amount associated with the Orange candidate is one dollar, if the Green candidate wins you will only receive 50 cents for that election, regardless of whether you voted for the Green or Orange candidate.

In the experiment each of you will be assigned to one of three voter types. A voter type simply specifies for each voter the monetary amount associated with each candidate. Consider the following payoff schedule. (Note: this is just an example, not the actual payoffs you will see during the experiment.)

	Orange	Blue	Green	Number of Voters
Type 1	1.00	.50	.25	8
Type 2	.25	.50	1.00	5
Type 3	1.00	.50	.50	4

In this case, if you are assigned to be a type 1 voter, the Orange candidate yields a higher payoff than the Blue candidate does, and the Blue candidate yields a higher payoff than the Green candidate. If you are assigned to be a type 2 voter then the Green candidate yields a higher payoff than the Blue candidate does, and the Blue candidate yields a higher payoff than the Orange candidate. And if you are assigned to be a type 3 voter, the Orange candidate yields a higher payoff than the Blue and Green candidates, who each have identical payoffs. During the experiment, you will know your type, but you will not know which subjects have been assigned to the other types. However, you will know the number of voters that have been assigned to a particular type. This number is displayed in the fifth column above. In this example there are eight type 1 voters, five type 2 voters and four type 3 voters.

Using the example above, if we were to hold an election which candidate would win? The candidate that receives the most votes. That is, suppose all voters vote for candidate Green, then Green would receive 17 votes and win. Alternatively, if Green receives 6 votes, Orange receives 7 votes, and Blue receives 3 votes, Orange would be the winner. Suppose that Blue and Orange both receive 6 votes and Green receive 5 votes? Then the computer will randomly choose who is the winner between Blue and Orange.

Again, let me summarize the events thus far. Each of you will be assigned to one of three voter types. You will know your type, and number of voters within the three type categories. Your type determines the monetary amounts associated with each of the three candidates. An election will be held, and you will be required to vote for one of the three candidates. You will receive the monetary amount associated with the winning candidate.

Voting Groups.   First, we will divide you into two groups. One group will be called group A, and the other will be called group B. You will know your assigned group, but you will not know the group other subjects have been assigned to. However, you will know the number of voters assigned within each group. The reason we have divided you into two groups is because you will be voting sequentially. First, all members of group A will vote for the candidates. The results of the election will be revealed to voters in both groups, then group B voters will vote. In effect we will have two elections, one where group A votes and a second where group B votes. However, the winning candidate will be determined by tallying the votes across the two elections. Consider the new payoff schedule below. This is the same payoff schedule we used above, but now voters have been divided into two groups (the last two columns). In group A there are eight voters and in group B there are nine. Also notice that within group A, four voters have type 1 preferences, three voters have type 2 preferences, and one voter has a type 3 preference.

	Orange	Blue	Green	Number of Voters	Group A	Group B
Type 1	1.00	.50	.25	8	4	4
Type 2	.25	.50	1.00	5	3	2
Type 3	1.00	.50	.50	4	1	3

Now let us consider how election results are computed again. Consider the first stage, where only group A voters cast ballots. There are eight voters in group A. Suppose all group A voters vote for Green; that is, Green receives eight votes from group A, and Blue and Orange receive zero votes from group A. But Green is not necessarily the winner in the election. The winner will depend also on how group B votes. There are nine voters in group B. Suppose that all nine voters vote for Blue. Then Blue would be the winner, receiving nine votes to Green's eight.

Here is a more complicated example: Suppose group A votes as follows: Orange receives three votes, Blue two, and Green three. Then suppose group B votes as follows: Orange receives three votes, Blue five, and Green one. Of the seventeen total votes, then, Orange has received six, Blue has received seven, and Green has received four. Because Blue has received the most votes across both groups, Blue is the winner even though Blue received the least votes in group A. What matters is which candidate receives the most votes from the total across the two groups. Suppose that two of the candidates are tied in total votes across both groups. Then, the computer will randomly choose who is the winner between the two tied candidates.

Information about the Candidates. The second complication is the most important. In the payoff schedule above you knew how each of the three candidates associated with your respective payoff. That is, if you were a type 1 voter, you knew the Orange candidate was worth one dollar, the Blue candidate was worth 50 cents, and the Green candidate was worth 25 cents. In this experiment you will not be given this information. During the experiment you will be voting for either the Orange, Blue, or Green candidates, however you will not know which candidate is associated with which payoff. Instead you will see the following payoff schedule (note that as opposed to previous payoff schedules this payoff schedule has different monetary amounts, and the number of voters has been altered).

Payoff Matrix

	x	y	z	Number of Voters	Group A	Group B
Type 1	1.00	.50	.25	12	6	6
Type 2	.25	.50	1.00	12	6	6
Type 3	.25	1.00	.50	12	6	6

The Orange candidate could either be type x, y, or z. Similarly, the Green and Blue candidates could either be type x, y, or z. You may wonder at this point how you may figure out which candidate is associate with which payoff (or type). First, before each election, voters in group A will be told the identity of one candidate. They will be told, for example, that the Orange candidate is either type x, y, or z. Hence, group A's problem is to determine the identity of the remaining two candidates. Note that you will participate in several rounds of this experiment, and in each round the computer will randomly reveal the identity of one candidate. So for example in one round it might be the Green candidate is z, and in the next it might be that the Orange candidate is y, or any possible combination. Also note that candidate identities and types are mutually exclusive. Candidate will never be assigned the same type. That is, if the Green candidate is z, and the Blue candidate is x, then it must be the case that the Orange candidate is y. Thus, there will never be a case, for example, where the Green and Blue candidate are both assigned to type y.

After group A has made their voting decision, the results will be revealed in the two history boxes (some hypothetical numbers have been inserted for group A):

Election Results by Type

	Type 1			Type 2			Type 3		
	O	B	G	O	B	G	O	B	G
Group A	0	3	3	6	0	0	2	2	2
Group B									
Total									

Election Results by Group

	O	B	G
Group A	8	5	5
Group B			
Total			

The first history box is just the voting results broken down by types. The next history box breaks the voting results down by groups. Notice, in the first history box, type 1 voters in group A split between the Blue and Green candidate. Type 2 voters in Group A all voted for the Orange candidate, and type 3 voters were evenly split among the three candidates. This information is aggregated in the second history box. Notice in the first stage the Orange candidate has a three-vote lead.

After this information is displayed, it is group B's turn to vote. Prior to casting a ballot, voters within Group B will be told the identity of another candidate. This will be a different candidate than the one revealed to group A. The computer will randomly reveal the identity of one of the two remaining candidates. Again the task for group B is to determine which candidate is associated with what type. Before group B votes, information about the voting results of group A will be revealed in the history box.

After group B casts their ballots, the votes from both elections will be tallied and the winning candidate will be announced. In the case of a tie between candidates, the computer program randomly selects a winner. Your display will reveal the following information. (Group B's votes have been assigned arbitrarily.) Your display will also reveal the winning candidate and your payoff (a hypothetical payoff is included below).

Election Results by Type

	Type 1			Type 2			Type 3		
	O	B	G	O	B	G	O	B	G
Group A	0	3	3	6	0	0	2	2	2
Group B	2	2	2	2	2	2	2	2	2
Total	2	5	5	8	2	2	4	4	4

Election Results by Group

	O	B	G
Group A	8	5	5
Group B	6	6	6
Total	14	11	11

THE WINNING CANDIDATE IS 'O'; YOU RECEIVE A PAYOFF OF 25 CENTS.

After the final results have been announced, your payoff for that period will be recorded in a running tally (this will be displayed on your computer screen). We will then repeat this process for an undetermined number of periods. You will not be told how many elections we will have. After completion of the experiment, your payoffs will be tallied, and you will be paid in cash your accumulated earnings. Note that we will play several rounds of this experiment. In each round you will be randomly assigned to either group A or group B, and you will be randomly assigned to one of the three voter types.

Let me summarize the sequence of events. (1) You will be randomly assigned to either group A or group B; (2) You will be randomly assigned to one of the three voter types; (3) Group A will be told the identity of one candidate; (4) Group A will be asked to vote for one of the three candidates; (5) After group A votes, the results will be revealed in a history box; (6) Group B will be told the identity of one of the remaining two unknown candidates; (7) Group B will be asked to vote for one of the three candidates; (8) The totals from the two elections will be tallied; (9) A winner is announced, and you receive a payoff from the winning candidate; (10) Repeat the process at (1).

Subject Number

Quiz

T   F   1. You get paid based on who you voted for not who wins the election.

T   F   2. The winning candidate is the candidate who wins the most votes in group A.

T   F   3. If Blue is revealed to be candidate x, then Orange cannot be candidate x.

T   F   4. If Green is revealed to be candidate y, then Blue must be candidate x.

T   F   5. If voters in group A are told that Blue is, for example, candidate x, then voters in group B are also given the same information about candidate Blue.

T   F   6. In each election your voter type and group will stay exactly the same.

Estimated Equations in Chapters 7 and 8

TABLE D1. Electoral Success of Candidate *y* (Moderate) Logit (Sequential versus Simultaneous Voting)

	Coefficient	Standard Error	z	$p > |z|$
Sequential voting (0 for simultaneous voting, 1 for sequential voting—in baseline sequential voting *y* is unrevealed)	1.32	0.60	2.21	0.03
Period (1–25)	0.04	0.02	1.85	0.06
Low α (0 for high α, 1 for low α)	−0.60	0.31	−1.91	0.06
y revealed to simultaneous voters (1 for *y* revealed to simultaneous voters, 0 otherwise)	4.46	1.15	3.90	0.00
y revealed to early sequential voters (1 for *y* revealed to group A voters in sequential voting, 0 otherwise)	2.37	0.43	5.55	0.00
y revealed to later sequential voters (1 for *y* revealed to group B voters in sequential voting, 0 otherwise)	0.18	0.40	0.44	0.66
Low information in sequential (1 for low-information group B voters in sequential voting, 0 otherwise)	−0.85	0.33	−2.54	0.01
Constant	−1.90	0.59	−3.22	0.00
Number of observations	250			
Log of likelihood function	−126.21			
Pseudo R^2	0.27			
Percent correctly classified	75.20			

Note: Null case is liberal or conservative revealed in a simultaneous voting election and α high; ties are coded as 0.5.

TABLE D2. **Voting for Least Preferred Candidate Logit**

	Coefficient	Standard Error	z	$p > |z|$
Later voter high-information				
(1 for high-information voter in group B in				
sequential voting, 0 for otherwise)	−0.39	0.12	−3.16	0.00
Later voter low-information				
(1 for low-information voter in group B in				
sequential voting, 0 for otherwise)	0.30	0.11	2.76	0.01
Period				
(1–25)	−0.02	0.01	−3.92	0.00
Low α*				
(0 for high α, 1 for low α)	0.64	0.09	7.22	0.00
Moderate voter				
(1 for voter of type 2, 0 otherwise)	3.61	0.13	27.02	0.00
y revealed to voter				
(1 for y directly revealed to the voter, either				
in simultaneous voting or in the voter's				
group in sequential voting, 0 otherwise)	2.00	0.12	16.21	0.00
Moderate voter* y revealed to voter				
(1 for voter type 2 and y revealed to voter,				
0 otherwise)	−4.29	0.23	−18.31	0.00
Constant	−3.60	0.14	−24.90	0.00
Number of observations	6000			
Log of likelihood function	−1753.25			
Pseudo R^2	0.23			
Percent correctly classified	87.50			

Note: Null case is early voter or simultaneous voter with α high and moderate unrevealed.

*We also estimated a model with Early Voter interacted with Low α, but the interactive term was insignificant.

TABLE D3. Electoral Success of Candidate *x* (Liberal Candidate) in Sequential Voting Elections Logit

	Coefficient	Standard Error	z	$p > |z|$
Low information				
(1 for low information voters in group B, 0 for otherwise)	0.48	0.43	1.12	0.26
Period				
(1–25)	−0.02	0.03	−0.84	0.40
Low α				
(0 for high α, 1 for low α)	0.57	0.44	1.32	0.19
Nonrepresentative early voters				
(1 for voter sequential 2, 0 for sequential 1)	−0.56	0.57	−0.98	0.33
x revealed to early voters				
(1 for *x* revealed to group A, 0 otherwise)	4.61	1.10	4.18	0.00
x revealed to early voters* nonrepresentative early voters				
(1 for *x* revealed to Group A and sequential voting, 0 otherwise)	2.51	.92	2.72	0.01
z revealed to early voters				
(1 for *z* revealed to group A, 0 otherwise)	3.41	1.05	3.24	0.00
Constant	−4.38	1.15	−3.81	0.00
Number of observations	200			
Log of likelihood function	−69.15			
Pseudo R^2	0.4548			
Percent correctly classified	83.50			

Note: Null case is *y* revealed to Group A, Sequential 1, and α high.

TABLE D4. Electoral Success of Candidate *y* (Moderate Candidate) Logit by Sequential Voting Election Type

	Coefficient	Standard Error	z	$p > |z|$
Representative early voters				
(0 simultaneous voting, 1 sequential 1)	1.29	0.62	2.09	0.04
Nonrepresentative early voters				
(0 simultaneous voting, 1 sequential 2)	1.34	0.62	2.16	0.03
Period				
(1–25)	0.04	0.02	1.85	0.07
Low α				
(0 for high α, 1 for low α)	−0.60	0.31	−1.91	0.06
y revealed to simultaneous voters				
(1 *y* revealed to simultaneous voters, 0 otherwise)	4.46	1.15	3.90	0.00
y revealed to early sequential voters				
(1 *y* revealed to group A, 0 otherwise)	2.37	0.43	5.54	0.00
y revealed to later sequential voters				
(1 *y* revealed to group B, 0 otherwise)	0.17	0.40	0.44	0.66
Low information in sequential				
(1 low-information group B, 0 otherwise)	−0.85	0.33	−2.53	0.01
Constant	−1.90	0.59	−3.22	0.00
Number of observations	250			
Log of likelihood function	−126.20			
Pseudo R^2	0.27			
Percent correctly classified	74.00			

TABLE D5. Voting for Least Preferred Candidate Logit

	Coefficient	Standard Error	z	$p > |z|$
Later voter high-information in representative (1 for high-information voter in group B in sequential 1, 0 for otherwise)	−1.13	0.20	−5.54	0.000
Later voter low-information in representative (1 for low-information voter in group B in sequential 1, 0 for otherwise)	0.23	0.15	1.62	0.11
Period (1–25)	−0.02	0.01	−3.91	0.00
Low α* (0 for high α, 1 for low α)	0.64	0.09	7.20	0.00
Moderate voter (1 for voter of type 2, 0 otherwise)	3.63	0.13	27.07	0.00
y revealed to voter (1 for y directly revealed to the voter, either in simultaneous voting or in the voter's group in sequential voting, 0 otherwise)	1.98	0.12	16.09	0.00
Moderate voter* y revealed to voter (1 for voter type 2 and y revealed to voter, 0 otherwise)	−4.32	0.24	−18.37	0.00
Later voter in nonrepresentative (1 for later voter in sequential 2, 0 otherwise)	0.23	0.11	2.16	0.03
Constant	−3.60	0.14	−24.86	0.00
Number of observations	6000			
Log of likelihood function	−1739.14			
Pseudo R^2	0.24			
Percent correctly classified	87.43			

Note: Null case is early voter or simultaneous voter with α high and moderate unrevealed.

Notes

Chapter 1

1. See Murphy 1998.

2. However, because California's new blanket primary law, which allows voters to vote in a party's primary even if they are not members of the party, is contrary to national party rules, which require that voting be restricted to party members, the legislature passed an amendment allowing for a double-counting procedure where votes from party members are the only ones that count in determining delegate allocations. See Gerber and Morton 1998 for a discussion of open versus closed primaries.

3. Guy Kelly, "Mail-in Ballots Have Big Effect on Campaigns," *Rocky Mountain News,* November 2, 1997, wysiwyg://93/http://insidedenver.com/extra/election/1102elec1.html

4. See Lois Romano, "Growing Use of Mail Voting Puts Its Stamp On Campaigns, Early Voters Are Targeted, Reducing Election Day Focus," *Washington Post,* November 29, 1998, A1, col. 5.

5. Richard Sammon, Colorado Daily on-line, Scripps Howard News Service, August 29, 1997, http://ben.boulder.co.us/media/colodaily/97/zaug29/VOTE29E.html

6. Chris Vetter, "Voting-by-mail Gains Support," the *Minnesota Daily Online,* October 28, 1996, http://www.daily.umn.edu/daily/1996/10/28/news/mail/

7. McCormick 1982.

8. The potential for fraud in early and mail-in balloting is another frequent criticism of these systems. In March 1998 a Florida judge threw out the November 4, 1997, Miami mayoral first-round election because of "a pattern of fraudulent, intentional and criminal conduct" in absentee balloting. Navarro 1998 reports: "In his written decision the judge said the absentee ballots cast in the election included those from people who did not vote, did not live in Miami or the district in which their ballot was cast, and did not qualify as unable to vote at the polls. Several ballots were even doctored to alter a vote for Carollo into for Saurez, the judge said." Advocates of mail-in and early balloting claim that with sufficient safeguards this sort of fraud will not occur. While our analysis does not address this issue specifically, we discuss some of the issues involving the tendency toward fraud in chapter 8.

9. In 1845 Congress enacted 3 U.S.C. Section 1: "The electors of President and Vice President shall be appointed, in each State, on the Tuesday next after the first Monday in November, in every fourth year succeeding every election of a President and Vice President."

10. In 1872 Congress enacted 2 U.S.C. Section 7: "The Tuesday after the first Mon-

day in November, in every even numbered year, is established as the day for the election, in each of the States and Territories of the United States of Representatives and Delegates to the Congress commencing on the 3rd day of January next hereafter."

11. While this first stage of the election process in nonpartisan elections is often called a "primary" election, technically it is not the same as a primary in partisan elections where the contest is over a particular party's nomination for the general election. Louisiana's first stage is part of the general election, which the Supreme Court recognized in declaring the Louisiana election date for the first stage unconstitutional.

12. Oregon's voting-by-mail and early voting system was recently unsuccessfully challenged as violating the congressional statute on the federal election day in Federal District Court, *Voting Integrity Project Inc., et al. v. Phil Keisling,* U.S. District Court Case No. CV98–1372. Since much voting does still take place on the federally mandated date, the court held that the procedure was constitutional.

Chapter 2

1. Only Florida Democrats held presidential primaries before 1956.

2. Palmer 1997, chapter 3, reviews much of this history. See also Ranney 1977.

3. There is federal regulation of campaign spending of presidential candidates, however, and these limitations can complicate the nomination process, as noted in chapter 8.

4. New Hampshire, Ohio, and West Virginia started presidential primaries in 1916, while Alabama's dates from 1924 to 1934, restarting in 1940.

5. New Hampshire's primary, for example, although instituted in 1916 did not allow voters to express preferences for presidential candidates in their delegate selections until 1949 (see Palmer 1997, 2).

6. Interestingly, gradually some Southern whites began to vote for and support Republican presidential candidates while maintaining a Democratic party identity at the state level.

7. For a discussion of the white primary cases see Bott 1991, 234–36.

8. The California legislature recently passed an amendment to allow the parties to count only party members' votes for allocating delegates while maintaining the open primary process. Legal experts are uncertain about the constitutionality of this legislation since the open primary law was passed by referendum and it is unclear if the legislature can amend the law.

9. The Supreme Court ruled in 1981 in *Democratic Party of United States v. Wisconsin ex rel. La Follette* that the national party could require that delegates be selected in a closed primary; that state laws did not supersede the national party's right of free association. Nevertheless, the Democratic party has not always enforced this rule, allowing states with traditional open presidential primaries to continue to hold them. The national Republican party allows both open and closed primaries, and a significant number of primaries are open. See Bott 1991, 366–67, and Epstein 1983, 233–35, for discussions of the La Follette case.

10. Although it was not till 1980 that most candidates understood the change in the

process. Candidates like Frank Church entered late or skipped New Hampshire like Scoop Jackson in 1976.

11. Abramson et. al. 1992 and Abramowitz 1989 find evidence supporting an expected utility model of voter choices in presidential primaries.

12. For other examples of Bayesian learning models see Achen 1992; Alvarez 1997; Bartels 1993; Husted, Kenny, and Morton 1996.

13. Iowa and New Hampshire actually violated the Democratic National Party rules in order to schedule primaries in advance of other New England states in 1984. Yet neither delegation was unseated at the convention. See Palmer 1997, 137–54, for a discussion of the intricate scheduling battles between the two states, the national party, and other states. Because of the complicated battle, the Democratic party subsequently led to exemptions for Iowa and New Hampshire in the subsequent electoral cycles, maintaining their first-in-the-nation status. Other states have challenged these states, notably Louisiana, Arizona, and Delaware in 1996.

14. However, as noted in the Introduction, they have attempted to induce states to spread primaries out in 2000, without success.

15. While New Hampshire has not needed to engage in front-loading, its actions and attempts to maintain its first-in-the-nation status are clearly similar to other states' attempts at front-loading. In 1975 the state enacted legislation to require that its primary be held either the second Tuesday in March or on the Tuesday immediately preceding the date on which any other New England state scheduled a similar election. This law was amended in 1995 to require that there be a gap of seven full days between New Hampshire's primary and any other primary. See Palmer 1997.

16. The Southern states that held primaries on Super Tuesday in 1988 were Texas, Florida, North Carolina, Georgia, Missouri, Virginia, Tennessee, Maryland, Louisiana, Alabama, Kentucky, Oklahoma, Mississippi, and Arkansas. Massachusetts and Rhode Island also held primaries on the same date, and Washington, Hawaii, Idaho, Nevada, and American Samoa held caucuses.

17. Ironically, some argue that the front-loaded system has made the earliest states, Iowa and New Hampshire, even more significant than before. Certainly, candidates appear to continue to spend considerable more time and resources in these two states than in others in the pre-primary season. Nevertheless, the shortening of the period of time between these states' contests and those of others makes it nearly impossible for a candidate to depend upon success in Iowa or New Hampshire as a principal method of building support among voters in the remaining states.

18. We thank Philip Paolino for suggesting this point. For discussions of the reform proposals see Ceasar 1982, 113–53, and Palmer 1997, 159–67, 175–79.

Chapter 3

1. See Amy Waldman, "While Ballots Trickle In, Rivals Wait," *New York Times,* November 7, 1998, and Amy Waldman, "Killing of Doctor Becomes a Factor in Political Races," *New York Times,* October 27, 1998.

2. See Steinbicker 1938.

3. See Bott 1991. The Federal Voting Assistance Act of 1955 and the Overseas Voting Rights Act of 1975 also required states to allow some citizens to register and vote absentee in federal elections.

4. Some states still have lengthy residency requirements for registration as party members and participation in closed primaries; for instance, in New York a voter must be a resident for one year in order to register to vote in a party's primary election.

5. Jonathan P. Hicks,"After Six Weeks, Vacco Concedes Attorney General Race to Spitzer," *New York Times,* December 15, 1998.

6. We thank Janet Box-Steffensmeier and Gary Jacobson for providing us with this data.

7. Larry Levine, private communication.

8. Larry Levine, private communication.

Chapter 4

1. Actually, Hotelling is not the first formal modeler of voting—we know that Condorcet preceded him in 1785. However, Hotelling's influence on formal models of voting is sizable. One of his students, Kenneth Arrow, has produced probably the most central result of social choice theory (his Impossibility Theorem), and two of Arrow's students have provided significant additions to Hotelling's original voting work—Anthony Downs and Roger Myerson. Downs's work clearly follows from Hotelling's model, and for this reason we call that approach Hotelling-Downsian. Myerson's work with Robert Weber serves as the basis for the voting model that we present in the next chapter.

2. Technically it is possible for voter preferences to be aligned in a symmetric way to ensure an equilibrium (see Hinich and Munger 1994). But this type of symmetric alignment is considered highly unlikely.

3. However, in order for an equilibrium to exist in some cases, actors must be using what game theorists call *mixed strategies* or a strategy of randomization in their choices. See Morrow 1994.

4. For a discussion of this concept and game theory in political science, see Morrow 1994.

5. This might be seen as counterintuitive—that is, in private consumption decisions, individuals rationally ignore information and make bad choices, but in collective decisions, where the connection between one's decision and the outcome is not solely dependent on one's own choice as in private consumption, the mistake is not made.

Chapter 5

1. Thinking of a model as a "story" has a long tradition among modelers—graduate students in economics are often struck by the constant question asked of presenters in seminars: "So what is your story here?" In contrast, graduate students in political science hear more often: "So what is your dependent variable here?" In this chapter we explain our story, and in the following two chapters we try to answer the second question. We thank Kelly Kadera for reminding us of the "story" view of models.

2. Ceasar 1982 notes that proposals for a national primary typically have a runoff requirement.

3. In the experiments, however, we do assume that our subjects selfishly maximize expected monetary payoffs, as we discuss in the next chapter.

4. An alternative way to think of the analysis is at the elite or "group" level of voting. That is, while at the individual level in extremely large elections strategic concerns may be insufficient to motivate voting choices, for a group of like-minded voters these concerns can be sizable as discussed in chapter 3.

5. One may also expect equilibria in which later voters "coordinate" their voting strategies from early outcomes. However, such coordination equilibria do not occur when later voters know different information from early voters, and later voters are therefore able to determine the entire distribution of candidate position from early voting and the information revealed to them. Therefore, coordination equilibria are not relevant in our analysis. We thank Roger Gordon for pointing out that coordination equilibria can occur.

Chapter 6

1. The experimental results presented in this chapter are also summarized in Morton and Williams 1999.

2. The mean difference is -0.24, with a standard error of 0.055 and a t-statistic of -4.45.

3. The mean difference is 0.09, with a standard error of 0.08 and a t-statistic of 1.15.

4. The mean difference is -0.15 in the percentage of wins, with a standard error of 0.07 and a t-statistic of -2.14.

5. The mean difference is 0.28, with a standard error of 0.09 and a t-statistic of 3.21.

6. The mean difference is 0.21, with a standard error of 0.16 and a t-statistic of 1.28.

7. The mean difference is 0.20, with a standard error of 0.06 and a t-statistic of 3.

8. The mean difference is 0.00, with a standard error of 0.09 and a t-statistic of 0.00.

9. The mean difference is -0.30, with a standard error of 0.07 and a t-statistic of -4.15.

10. We also estimated multinomial logits of voter choices (vote for x, y, or z), and the results were consistent with the logits reported here.

11. Of course as noted above even if early voters choose informatively the randomization of the voting process may not allow later voters to infer early voters' knowledge of the candidates.

12. The mean difference between the two equals $-.029$, with a standard error of 0.01 and a t-statistic of -2.64.

13. In this one election the conservative candidate is revealed to early voters, all conservative voters vote for him, the moderate voters split between the conservative and moderate candidates, and four out of the five moderate voters vote for the moderate candidate.

14. In 2.56 percent of the 6,000 voting choices voters knowingly voted for their least preferred candidate (that candidate was revealed to them), which we classified as a vot-

ing error. When we estimate a logit of the votes for a voter's least preferred candidate excluding those observations in which the voter knowingly voted for her least preferred candidate, we find that the variables LATER VOTER HIGH INFORMATION and LATER VOTER LOW INFORMATION are both significant and have the predicted negative and positive signs, respectively.

Chapter 7

1. Of course, extreme preferences do not necessarily mean that voters will vote purely ideologically. Stone and Abramowitz 1983 find that Iowa caucus participants care about electability as well as the candidates' policy positions. In our theoretical formulation electability is a matter of perception. If nonrepresentative early voters perceive that their favored candidate has little chance of winning, they too would vote strategically for another choice. However, since we assume that these voters only know the identity of one of the candidates, strategic voting for these reasons is not rational. If we were to increase the number of candidates in the model and allow early voters greater knowledge of the candidates, then this type of strategic voting by early voters would be rational.

2. In unreported comparison-of-means tests only when α is low and later voters have detailed information is there a difference in the number of wins by y that is barely significant with a t-statistic of 1.48.

3. The t-statistic is 2.35.

4. That is, x is revealed to A and y is revealed to B, which occurred in 20 elections in Sequential 2 and 16 elections in Sequential 1; the t-statistic is 3.98.

5. We also estimated logits with dummy variables for other possible candidate revelations, but these variables were insignificant.

Chapter 8

1. James Dao, "Bradley and Gore Competing for Donations in New Jersey," *New York Times,* March 7, 1999.

2. See Mireya Navarro, "Citing Fraud, Judge Invalidates Miami Mayoral Election," *New York Times,* March 5, 1998.

3. Most argue that the secret ballot was a de facto literacy test and that this was the cause of the decrease in turnout. Heckelman contends that the secret ballot used symbols to help the illiterate, and the real effect was a decline in bribery.

Appendix A

1. For a detailed discussion of formal versus nonformal models, see Morton 1999.

2. For a more expanded discussion of these issues, see chapter 4 of Morton 1999.

References

Abramowitz, Alan I. 1989. "Viability, Electability, and Candidate Choice in a Presidential Primary Election: A Test of Competing Models." *Journal of Politics* 51 (November): 977–92.

Abramowitz Alan I., and Walter J. Stone. 1983. "Winning May Not Be Everything, But It's More than We Thought: Presidential Party Activists in 1980." *American Political Science Review* 77 (December): 945–56.

Abramowitz, Alan I., and Walter J. Stone. 1984. *Nomination Politics: Party Activists and Presidential Choice.* New York: Praeger.

Abramson, Paul R., John H. Aldrich, and David W. Rohde. 1998. *Change and Continuity in the 1996 Elections.* Washington, D.C.: CQ Press.

Abramson, Paul R., John H. Aldrich, Phil Paolino, and David W. Rohde. 1992. "'Sophisticated' Voting in the 1988 Presidential Primaries." *American Political Science Review* 86 (March): 55–69.

Achen, Christopher H. 1992. "Breaking to Iron Triangle: Social Psychology, Demographic Variables, and Linear Regression in Voting Research." *Political Behavior* 14:195–211.

Aldrich, John H. 1980a. *Before the Convention.* Chicago: University of Chicago Press.

———. 1980b. "A Dynamic Model of Presidential Nomination Campaigns." *American Political Science Review* 74 (September): 651–69.

———. 1993. "Rational Choice and Turnout." *American Journal of Political Science* 20 (February): 246–78.

Aldrich, John, and Forrest D. Nelson. 1984. *Linear Probability, Logit, and Probit Models.* Beverly Hills, Calif.: Sage.

Alesina, Alberto. 1987. "Macroeconomics Policy in a Two-Party System as a Repeated Game." *Quarterly Journal of Economics* 102:651–78.

Alvarez, R. Michael. 1997. *Information and Elections.* Ann Arbor: University of Michigan Press.

Alvarez, R. Michael, and Garrett Glasgow. 1997. "Do Voters Learn from Presidential Election Campaigns?" Working paper, California Institute of Technology.

Ansolabehere, Stephen, Shanto Iyengar, Adam Simon, and N. Valentino. 1994. "Do Negative Campaigns Demobilize the Electorate?" *American Political Science Review* 84 (September): 829–38.

Austen-Smith, David. 1987. "Interest Groups, Campaign Contributions and Probabilistic Voting." *Public Choice* 54 (2): 123–39.

———. 1992. "Explaining the Vote: Constituency Constrains on Sophisticated Voting." *American Journal of Political Science* 36 (February): 68–95.

161

Austen-Smith, David, and Jeffrey Banks. 1996. "Information Aggregation, Rationality, and the Condorcet Jury Theorem." *American Political Science Review* 90 (March): 34–45.

Balz, Dan. 1993. "California Moves Up '96 Primary to March." *Washington Post,* October 6, A3.

Banerjee, Abhijit V. 1992. "A Simple Model of Herd Behavior." *Quarterly Journal of Economics* 107 (August): 797–818.

Baron, David P. 1989. "A Noncooperative Theory of Legislative Coalitions." *American Journal of Political Science* 35 (February): 57–90.

Baron, David, and John Ferejohn. 1989. "Bargaining in Legislatures." *American Political Science Review* 89 (December): 1181–1206.

Bartels, Larry M. 1988. *Presidential Primaries and the Dynamics of Public Choice.* Princeton: Princeton University Press.

———. 1993. "Messages Received: The Political Impact of Media Exposure." *American Political Science Review* 87 (June): 267–85.

Berg, Sven. 1993. "Condorcet Jury Theorem, Dependency among Jurors." *Social Choice and Welfare* 10 (January): 87–95.

Berinksky, Adam, Nancy Burns, and Michael Traugott. 1998. "Who Votes By Mail? A Dynamic Model of the Individual-Level Consequences of Vote-by-Mail Systems." Working paper, Center for Political Studies, University of Michigan.

Besley, Timothy, and Stephen Coate. 1997. "An Economic Model of Representative Democracy." *Quarterly Journal of Economics* 112 (February): 85–114.

Bikhchandani, Sushil, David Hirshleifer, and Ivo Welch. 1992. "A Theory of Fads, Fashions, Custom, and Cultural Change as Information Cascades." *Journal of Political Economy* 100 (October): 992–1026.

Bott, Alexander J. 1990. *Handbook of United States Election Laws and Practices: Political Rights.* New York: Greenwood Press.

Brady, Henry E. 1996. "Strategy and Momentum in Presidential Primaries." In *Political Analysis,* vol. 5, ed. John R. Freeman. Ann Arbor: University of Michigan Press.

Brady, Henry E., and Stephen Ansolabehere. 1989. "The Nature of Utility-Functions in Mass Publics." *American Political Science Review* 83 (March): 143–63.

Brians, Craig L., and Martin P. Wattenberg. 1996. "Campaign Issue Knowledge and Salience: Comparing Reception from TV Commercials, TV News, and Newspapers." *American Journal of Political Science* 40 (February): 172–93.

Buell, Emmett H., Jr. 1991. "Meeting Expectations? Major Newspaper Coverage of Candidates During the 1988 Exhibition Season." In *Nominating the President,* ed. Emmett H. Buell Jr. and Lee Sigelman, 150–95. Knoxville: University of Tennessee Press.

Calderia, Gregory A., and Samuel C. Patterson. 1985. "Mailing In the Vote: Correlates and Consequences of Absentee Voting." *American Journal of Political Science* 29 (November): 766–88.

Caldeira Gregory A., Samuel C. Patterson, and Gregory A. Markko. 1985. "The Mobilization of Voters in Congressional Elections." *Journal of Politics* 47 (June): 490–509.

Calvert, Randall L. 1985. "The Value of Biased Information: A Rational Choice Model of Political Advice." *Journal of Politics* 47 (June): 530–55.

———. 1986. *Models of Imperfect Information in Politics.* Chur, Switzerland: Harwood Academic Publishers.

Cameron, Charles M., and James M. Enelow. 1992. "Asymmetric Policy Effects, Campaign Contribution, and the Spatial Theory of Elections." *Mathematical and Computer Modeling* 16:117–32.

Cameron, Charles M., and J. Jung. 1992. "Strategic Endorsements." Working Paper, Department of Political Science, Columbia University, New York.

Ceasar, James W. 1982. *Reforming the Reforms: A Critical Analysis of the Presidential Selection Process.* Cambridge, Mass.: Ballinger.

Collier, Kenneth E., Peter C. Ordeshook, and Kenneth C. Williams. 1989. "The Rationally Uninformed Electorate: Some Experimental Evidence." *Public Choice* 53: 101–30.

Condorcet, M.J.A.N.C., Marquis de. 1785. *Essai sur l'Application de l'Analyse la Probabilité des Decisions Rendues la Pluralité des Voix.* Paris: l'Imprimerie Royale.

Cook, Rhodes. 1989. "The Nominating Process." In *The Elections of 1988,* ed. Michael Nelson. Washington, D.C.: Congressional Quarterly Press.

———. 1997. "CQ Roundtable: GOP Wants a Revamp of Primary Process." *Congressional Quarterly,* August 9: p. 1942.

Cooper, Alexandra, and Michael C. Munger. 1996. "The (Un)Predictability of Presidential Primaries with Many Candidates: Some Simulation Evidence." Presented at the annual meeting of the American Political Science Association, San Francisco.

Cox, Gary W. 1997. *Making Votes Count: Strategic Coordination in the World's Electoral Systems.* Cambridge: Cambridge University Press.

Cremer Jacques, and Thomas R. Palfrey. 1999. "Political Confederation." *American Political Science Review* 93 (March): 69–83.

Dekel, Eddie, and Michele Piccione. 1997. "The Equivalence of Simultaneous and Sequential Binary Elections." Working paper, Department of Economics, Northwestern University.

Delli Carpini, Michael X. 1984. "Scooping the Voters? The Consequences of the Networks' Early Call of the 1980 Presidential Race." *Journal of Politics* 46 (August): 866–85.

Downs, Anthony. 1957. *An Economic Theory of Democracy.* New York: Harper and Row.

Epstein, Leon D. 1986. *Political Parties in the American Mold.* Madison: University of Wisconsin Press.

Erikson, Robert S., Gerald C. Wright, and John P. McIver. 1993 . *Statehouse Democracy: Public Opinion and Policy in the American States.* Cambridge: Cambridge University Press.

Faber, Ronald J., and M. Claire Storey. 1984. "Recall of Information from Political Advertisements." *Journal of Advertising* 13 (3): 39–44.

Feddersen, Timothy J., and Wolfgang Pesendorfer. 1996. "The Swing Voter's Curse." *American Economic Review* 86 (June): 408–24.

———. 1998. "Convicting the Innocent: The Inferiority of Unanimous Jury Verdicts under Strategic Voting." *American Political Science Review* 92 (March): 23–35.

Fey, Mark. 1996. "Informational Cascades, Sequential Elections, and Presidential Primaries." Paper presented at the annual meeting of the American Political Science Association in San Francisco.

Filer, John, Lawrence Kenny, and Rebecca Morton. 1993. "Redistribution, Income, and Voting." *American Journal of Political Science* 37 (February): 63–87.

Fiorina, Morris. 1995, " Rational Choice and the New (Questionable) Institutionalism." *Polity* 28 (fall): 107–15.

Garramone, Gina M. 1984. "Voter Responses to Negative Political Ads." *Journalism Quarterly* 61:250–59.

———. 1985. "Motivation and Selective Attention to Political Information Formats." *Journalism Quarterly* 62:37–44.

Geer, John Gray. 1989 *Nominating Presidents: An Evaluation of Voters and Primaries.* New York: Greenwood Press.

Gerber, Alan. 1996. "Rational Voters, Candidate Spending, and Incomplete Information: A Theoretical Analysis with Implications for Campaign Finance Reform." Working paper, Yale University, New Haven.

Gerber, Elisabeth R., and Rebecca B. Morton. 1998. "Primary Election Systems and Representation." *Journal of Law, Economics, and Organization* 14 (2): 304–24.

Gerber, Elisabeth R., Rebecca B. Morton, and Thomas A. Rietz. 1998. "Majority Requirements and Minority Representation." Working paper, University of Iowa.

Greer, John G. 1988. "Assessing the Representativeness of Electorates in Presidential Primaries." *American Journal of Political Science* 32 (November): 929–45.

Grofman, Bernard, and Scott L. Feld. 1988. "Rousseau's General Will: A Condorcetian Perspective." *American Political Science Review* 82 (June): 567–76.

Grossman, Gene M., and Elhanan Helpman. 1996. "Electoral Competition and Special Interest Politics." *Review of Economic Studies* 63 (April): 265–86.

Hadley, Arthur T. 1976. *The Invisible Primary.* Englewood Cliffs, N.J.: Prentice-Hall.

Hagen, Michael G. 1989. "Voter Turnout in Primary Elections." In *The Iowa Caucuses and the Presidential Nomination Process,* ed. Peverill Squire. Boulder: Westview Press.

Heckelman, Jac C. 1995. "The Effects of the Secret Ballot on Turnout Rates." *Public Choice* 28 (1–2): 107–24.

Hicks, Jonathan P. 1998. "After Six Weeks, Vacco Concedes Attorney General Race to Spitzer." *New York Times,* December 15.

Hinich, Melvin J., and Michael C. Munger. 1989. "Political Investment, Voter Perceptions, and Candidate Strategies: An Equilibrium Spatial Analysis." In *Models of Strategic Choice in Politics,* Peter C. Ordeshook, ed. 49–68. Ann Arbor: University of Michigan Press.

———. 1994. *Ideology and the Theory of Political Choice.* Ann Arbor: University of Michigan Press.

———. 1997. *Analytical Politics.* Cambridge: Cambridge University Press.

Hotelling, Harold. 1929. "Stability in Competition." *Economic Journal* 39 (March): 41–57.

Husted, Thomas, Lawrence Kenny, Rebecca B. Morton, and Christopher Waller. 1995. "Constituent Errors in Assessing Their Senators." *Public Choice* 83:251–71.

Iyengar, Shanto, and Stephen Ansolabehere. 1995. *Going Negative.* New York: Free Press.

Jackman, Robert W. 1993. "Response to Aldrich's 'Rational Choice and Turnout': Rationality and Political Participation." *American Journal of Political Science* 37 (February): 279–90.

Jackson, John E. 1983. "Election Night Reporting and Voter Turnout." *American Journal of Political Science* 27 (November): 615–35.

Jewell, Malcolm E. 1984. *Parties and Primaries: Nominating State Governors.* New York: Praeger.

Just, Marion, Ann Crigler, and Lori Wallach. 1990. "Thirty Seconds or Thirty Minutes: What Viewers Learn from Spot Advertisements and Candidate Debates." *Journal of Communication* 40 (3): 120–33.

Keefe, William J. 1998. *Parties, Politics, and Public Policy in America,* 8th ed. Washington, D.C.: CQ Press.

Keeter, Scott, and Cliff Zukin. 1983. *Uninformed Choice: The Failure of the New Presidential Nominating System.* New York: Praeger.

Kelly, Guy. 1997. "Mail-in Ballots Have Big Effect on Campaigns." *Rocky Mountain News,* November 2. http://insidedenver.com/extra/election/1102elect1.html

Kettleborough, Charles. 1917. "Absent Voting." *American Political Science Review* 11 (May): 320–22.

Kenney, Patrick, and Tom W. Rice. 1994. "The Psychology of Political Momentum." *Political Research Quarterly* 47:923–38.

Kessel, John H. 1988. *Presidential Campaign Politics,* 3d ed. Chicago: Dorsey Press.

King, Gary. 1993. "The Methodology of Presidential Research." In *Researching the Presidency: Vital Questions, New Approaches,* ed. George C. Edwards III, John H. Kessel, and Bert A. Rockman, 387–414. Pittsburgh: University of Pittsburgh Press.

Kousser, J. Morgan. 1974. *The Shaping of Southern Politics: Suffrage Restriction and the Establishment of the One-Party South, 1880–1910.* New Haven: Yale University Press.

Ladha, Krishna K. 1992. "The Condorcet Jury Theorem, Free Speech, and Correlated Votes." *American Journal of Political Science* 36 (August): 617–34.

Ledyard, John O. 1984. "The Pure Theory of Large Two-Candidate Elections." *Public Choice* 44:7–41.

Los Angeles Times. 1998. "Senate Approves Moving Presidential Primary up to March." May 15.

Magleby, David B. 1987. "Participation in Mail Ballot Elections." *Western Political Quarterly* 40 (1): 79–91.

Marshall, Thomas R. 1981. *Presidential Nominations in a Reform Age.* New York: Praeger. (Copublished with the Eagleton Institute of Politics, Rutgers University.)

McCormick, Richard P. 1982. *The Presidential Game: The Origins of American Presidential Politics.* New York: Oxford University Press.

McGraw, Kathleen, Rebecca B. Morton, and Kenneth C. Williams. Forthcoming. *Experimental Methods in Political Science.* Ann Arbor: University Of Michigan Press.

McKelvey, Richard D., and Peter C. Ordeshook. 1985. "Elections with Limited Information: A Fulfilled Expectations Model Using Contemporaneous Poll and Endorsement Data as Information Sources." *Journal of Economic Theory* 36:55–85.

———. 1986. "Information, Electoral Equilibria, and the Democratic Ideal." *Journal of Politics* 48 (November): 909–37.

McLennan Andrew. 1998. "Consequences of the Condorcet Jury Theorem for Beneficial Information Aggregation by Rational Agents." *American Political Science Review* 92 (June): 413–18.

Merritt, Sharyne. 1984. "Negative Political Advertising: Some Empirical Findings." *Journal of Advertising* 13 (3): 27–38.

Miller, George Frederick. 1948. *Absentee Voters and Suffrage Laws.* Washington, D.C.: Daylion.

Miller, Nicholas. 1986. "Information, Electorates, and Democracy: Some Extensions and Interpretations of the Condorect Jury Theory." In *Information Pooling and Group Decision Making,* ed. Bernard Grofman and Guillermo Owen. Greenwich, Conn.: JAI Press.

Morrow, James D. 1994. *Game Theory for Political Scientists.* Princeton: Princeton University Press.

Morton, Rebecca B. 1987. "A Group Majority Voting Model of Public Good Provision." *Social Choice and Welfare* 4:117–31.

———. 1991. "Groups in Rational Turnout Models." *American Journal of Political Science* 3 (August): 758–76.

———. 1999. *Methods and Models: A Guide to the Empirical Analysis of Formal Models in Political Science.* Cambridge: Cambridge University Press.

Morton, Rebecca B., and Kenneth C. Williams. 1999. "Information Asymmetries and Simultaneous versus Sequential Voting," *American Political Science Review* 93 (March): 51–67.

Murphy, Margaret. 1998. "Secretary of State Pushes for Presidential Primary." Missouri Digital News, State Government Reporting Program, http://www.mdn.org/1998/stories/primary.htm (February 2).

Myerson, Roger B., and Robert J. Weber. 1993. "A Theory of Voting Equilibria." *American Political Science Review* 87 (March): 102–14.

Navarro, Mireya. 1998. "Citing Fraud, Judge Invalidates Miami Mayoral Election." *New York Times,* March 5.

Norrander, Barbara. 1989. "Ideological Representativeness of Presidential Primary Voters." *American Journal of Political Science* 33 (August): 570–87.

———. 1993. "Nomination Choices: Caucus and Primary Outcomes, 1976–88." *American Journal of Political Science* 37 (May): 343–64.

Oliver, J. Eric. 1996. "Who Votes at Home? The Influence of State Law and Party Activity on Absentee Voting and Overall Turnout." *American Journal of Political Science* 40 (May): 498–513.

Olson, Mancur. 1965. *The Logic of Collective Action.* Cambridge, Mass.: Harvard University Press.

Osborne Martin J., and Alan Slivinski. 1996. "A Model of Political Competition with Citizen-Candidates." *Quarterly Journal of Economics* 111 (February): 65–96.

Palfrey, Thomas R., and Keith T. Poole. 1987. "The Relationship between Information, Ideology, and Voting Behavior." *American Journal of Political Science* 31 (August): 511–30.

Palfrey, Thomas, and Howard Rosenthal. 1983. "A Strategic Calculus of Voting." *Public Choice* 41 (1): 7–53.

———. 1985. "Voter Participation and Strategic Uncertainty." *American Political Science Review* 79 (March): 62–78.

Palmer, Niall. 1997. *The New Hampshire Primary and the American Electoral Process.* Westport, Conn.: Praeger.

Paolino, Philip. 1996. "Perceptions of Candidate Viability: Media Effects During the Presidential Nomination Process." Presented at the annual meetings of the American Political Science Association, San Francisco.

———. 1998. "Voters' Perceptions of Candidate Viability: Uncertainty and the Prospects for Momentum." Presented at the annual meetings of the Midwest Political Science Association, Chicago.

Patterson, Thomas E. 1980. *The Mass Media Election: How Americans Choose Their President.* New York: Praeger.

Polsby, Nelson W. 1983. *Consequences of Party Reform.* New York: Oxford University Press.

Popkin, Samuel L. 1991. *The Reasoning Voter.* Chicago: University of Chicago Press.

Potters, Jan, Randolph Sloof, and Frans van Winden. 1997. "Campaign Expenditures, Contributions and Direct Endorsements: The Strategic Use of Information and Money to Influence Voter Behavior." *European Journal of Political Economy* 13:31.

Prat, Andrea. 1997. "Campaign Advertising and Voter Welfare." Working Paper, Center for Economic Research, Tilburg University, Netherlands.

Ranney, Austin. 1977. *Participation in American Presidential Nominations, 1976.* Washington, D.C.: American Enterprise Institute for Public Policy Research.

Riker, William H. 1980. "Implications for Disequilibrium of Majority Rule for the Study of Institutions." *American Political Science Review* 74 (June): 432–46.

Riker, William H., and Peter Ordeshook. 1968. "A Theory of the Calculus of Voting." *American Political Science Review* 62 (March): 25–42.

Robinson, Michael J., and Margaret Sheehan. 1983. *Over the Wire and on TV: CBS and UPI in Campaign 80.* New York: Russell Sage Foundation.

Romano, Lois. 1998. "Growing Use of Mail Voting Puts Its Stamp on Campaigns: Early Voters Are Targeted, Reducing Election Day Focus." *Washington Post.* November 29, A1.

Rosenfield, Margaret. 1994. "Early Voting," *Innovations in Election Administration,* 9, April, National Clearinghouse on Election Administration, Federal Election Commission, Washington, D.C.

Rosenstone, Steven J., and John Mark Hansen. 1993. *Mobilization, Participation, and Democracy in America.* New York: Macmillan.

Roth, Alvin. 1995. "Introduction to Experimental Economics." In *The Handbook of Experimental Economics,* ed. John Kagel and Alvin Roth. Princeton: Princeton University Press.

Schmidt, Amy B., Lawrence W. Kenny, and Rebecca B. Morton. 1996. "Evidence on Electoral Accountability in the U.S. Senate: Are Faithful Agents Really Punished?" *Economic Inquiry* 34:545–67.

Schneider, William. 1997. "And Now the GOP Iis Rewriting Its Rules." *National Journal,* April 12, 734.

Shafer, Byron E. 1983. *Quiet Revolution: The Struggle for the Democratic Party and the Shaping of Post-Reform Politics.* New York: Russell Sage Foundation.

Shapiro, William. 1997. "Too Early—and Too Late—for 2000." *USA Today,* November 19.

Simon, Adam. 1998. "The Winning Message? Candidate Behavior, Campaign Discourse, and Democracy." Unpublished manuscript, University of Washington, Seattle.

Sloth, B. 1993. "The Theory of Voting and Equilibria in Non-Cooperative Games." *Games and Economic Behavior* 5 (1): 152–69.

Smolka, Richard G. 1982. "Election Legislation." In *The Book of the States 1982–1983,* 91–95. Lexington, Ky.: Council of State Governments.

Stein, Robert M. 1998. "Early Voting." *Public Opinion Quarterly* 62:57–69.

Stein, Robert M., and Patricia A. Garcia-Monet. 1997. "Voting Early, but Not Often." *Social Science Quarterly* 78:657–71.

Steinbicker, Paul G. 1938. "Absentee Voting in the United States." *American Political Science Review* 32 (October): 898–907.

Stone, Walter J., and Alan I. Abramowitz. 1983. "Winning May Not Be Everything, But It's More Than We Thought: Presidential Party Activists in 1980." *American Political Science Review* 77 (December): 945–56.

Stone, Walter J., Alan I. Abramowitz, and Ronald B. Rapoport. 1989. "How Representative Are the Iowa Caucuses." In *The Iowa Caucuses and the Presidential Nomination Process,* ed. Peverill Squire. Boulder: Westview Press.

Stone, Walter J., Ronald B. Rapoport, and Lonna Rae Atkeson. 1995. A Simulation Model of Presidential Nomination Choice." *American Journal of Political Science* 39 (February): 135–61.

Strumpf, Koleman. 1997. "Sequential Elections Contests: Strategic Effects Oppose Momentum in Presidential Primaries." Working Paper, Department of Economics, University of North Carolina.

Traugott, Michael W. 1997. "An Evaluation of Voting-by-Mail in Oregon." Prepared for the Workshop on Voting-by-Mail, University of Michigan and the League of Women Voters, Washington, D.C.

Uhlaner, Carole J. 1989. "Rational Turnout: The Neglected Role of Groups." *American Journal of Political Science* 33 (May): 390–422.

Vetter, Chris. 1996. "Voting-by-Mail Gains Support." *Minnesota Daily Online,* October 28, http://www.daily.umn.edu/daily/1996/10/28/news/mail/

Waldman, Amy. 1998a. "Killing of Doctor Becomes a Factor in Political Races." *New York Times,* October 27.

———. 1998b. "While Ballots Trickle In, Rivals Wait." *New York Times,* November 7.

Wilcox, Clyde. 1991. Financing the 1988 Prenomination Campaigns." In *Nominating a President in 1988,* ed. Emmett Buell and Lee Sigelman, 91–118. Knoxville: University of Tennessee Press.

Williams, Daniel C., Stephen J. Weber, Gordon A. Haaland, Ronald H. Mueller, and Robert E. Craig. 1976. "Voter Decisionmaking in a Primary Election: An Evaluation of Three Models of Choice." *American Journal of Political Science* 20 (February): 37–49.

Wilson, Woodrow. 1966. "First Annual Message." In *The State of the Union Messages of the Presidents, 1790–1966,* vol. 3, 2544–50. New York: Chelsea House.

Witt, J. 1997. "Herding Behavior in a Roll-Call Voting Game." Working paper, Department of Economics, University of Amsterdam.

Wittman, Donald A. 1977. "Candidates with Policy Preferences: A Dynamic Model." *Journal of Economic Theory* 14:180–98.

Young, Peyton H. 1988. "Condorcet's Theory of Voting." *American Political Science Review* 82 (December): 1231–44.

Index

Abramowitz, Alan I., 7, 16, 18, 32, 59, 157n, 160n
Abramson, Paul R., 70, 157n
Absentee voting, 35, 36, 38, 39, 40, 41, 44, 49, 50, 111
Abstention, 67, 127
Achen, Christopher H., 157n
Aldrich, John H., 7, 11, 16, 20, 42, 43, 59, 60, 70, 73, 75, 101, 125, 157n
Alesina, Alberto, 52
Alvarez, R. Michael, 3, 22, 25, 32, 58, 75, 157n
Ansolabehere, Stephen, 58, 60
Arrow, Kenneth, 158n
Atkeson, Lonna Rae, 66
Austen-Smith, David, 57, 58

Baird, Brian, 4, 126
Balz, Dan, 2
Banks, Jeffrey, 57
Baron, David P., 58, 130
Bartels, Larry M., 3, 20, 21, 23, 32, 60, 75, 157n
Bayesian updating, 124
Bayesian voting model, 22
Berg, Sven, 57
Berinksky, Adam, 44, 46, 111
Besley, Timothy, 54
Blanket Primaries, 14
Bott, Alexander J., 156n, 158n
Box-Steffensmeier, Janet, 158n
Bradley, Tom, 37
Brady, Bill, 125
Brady, Henry E., 7, 60
Branstad, Terry E., 37

Brians, Craig L., 58
Brown, Edmund, 37
Buchanan, Pat, 72
Buckley, James, 54, 55, 62, 68
Burns, Nancy, 44, 46, 111
Bush, George, 21
Bush, George W., 30, 74

Caldeira, Gregory A., 37, 44
Calvert, Randall L., 52, 57
Cameron, Charles M., 58, 59
Campaign contributions, 56, 57
Campaign spending, 58, 126
Carter, Jimmy, 3, 17, 23, 135
Caucuses, 11, 16, 18, 19, 25
Ceasar, James W., 12, 16, 157n, 159n
Chancellor, John, 78
Cheney, Dick, 2
Ciruli, Floyd, 3
Citizen-candidate model, 54, 56
Civil War, 35
Clinton, William J., 53, 78
Closed primaries, 15, 19
Coate, Stephen, 54
Collier, Kenneth E., 57
Condorcet Jury Theorem, 57–58
Condorcet, Marquis de, 57, 67
Conlin, Roxanne, 37
Conventions, 10–11, 15, 16
Cook, Rhodes, 2, 72
Cooper, Alexandra, 7
Costa, Jim, 1
Cox, Gary W., 54, 55, 56
Craig, Robert E., 66
Cremer, Jacques, 128